ENCOUNTERING SCRIPTURE

ENCOUNTERING SCRIPTURE

A scientist explores the Bible

John Polkinghorne

First published in Great Britain in 2010

Society for Promoting Christian Knowledge
36 Causton Street
London SW1P 4ST

British Library Cataloguing-in-Publication Data
A catalogue record for this book is available from the British Library

ISBN 978–0–281–06253–9

1 3 5 7 9 10 8 6 4 2

Typeset by Graphicraft Ltd, Hong Kong
Printed in Great Britain by JF Print

Produced on paper from sustainable forests

To my friends in the Parish of the Good Shepherd,
Cambridge

Contents

Introduction

Scripture has been very important to me in my Christian life. For more than sixty years I have read the Bible every day and when in middle life I was ordained as an Anglican priest, I undertook the welcome duty of saying the Daily Office. Every year this takes me through the whole of the New Testament, and a good deal of the Old Testament.

The Bible is in many ways a very complex book. The material in it was written over a period of about a thousand years and the process of compilation ended almost two thousand years ago. The biblical writings originated in a variety of contrasting cultures, all with world views different in many respects from our modern, scientifically influenced understanding. Often biblical writers took over stories and insights from earlier ages, modifying and developing them in ways that seemed appropriate to their own times and experience, producing a text that is many-layered like an archaeological site. Much that we read in the Bible may seem strange to us, particularly in the Old Testament, where there are stories of war and violence that trouble us by being presented as if they were fulfilments of the express will of God. Sometimes, when different writers are telling the story of the same events, as is often the case in the Gospels for instance, there are discrepancies of detail that make it clear that we are reading human compositions, and not the result of an inerrant divine dictation. Despite these problems, all of which I shall have to confront in what follows, there is great spiritual truth and beauty to be found in Scripture. Anyone who has listened to a performance of Handel's *Messiah*, where the text is drawn wholly from the Bible, will have caught a glimpse of the majestic power and hopeful promise that are to be found in the pages of Scripture. Moreover, without the New Testament we would know essentially nothing about Jesus Christ, one of the most striking and influential figures of all time and someone who is of dominant significance in the spiritual history of humankind. The Bible is an indispensable foundational source for Christian thinking.

I have written this little book in the hope that it will be helpful to those who are seeking a careful and thoughtful engagement with the Bible in their quest for a truthful understanding of the ways of God and the nature of spiritual reality, but who are not necessarily concerned to enter into an exhaustive academic study of these issues. I think of the book as a reconnaissance because I want to explore the landscape of Scripture in a manner that notes and takes seriously many of its features, both inspiring and perplexing, but which does not attempt to give an account of the whole biblical terrain. My concern will centre on carefully selected typical examples of what one will encounter on a journey through biblical territory. What I am seeking to offer is a series of insights that have helped me in my own engagement with the Bible, illustrating what I have to say by appropriate citations that raise the issues that I want to address, while not pretending to attain an encyclopedic completeness in what I have to say.

In reading Scripture we should expect to find both inspiration and information. Christianity is a historically oriented religion. Its foundational stories, Christians believe, are not simply symbolic tales given us to stir our imaginations, but are rooted in God's actual acts of self-disclosure, mediated through particular persons and events. Therefore there is an evidential aspect to what we are told in the Bible. Scripture offers us testimony that has to be evaluated in a careful and honest way when assessing the degree of historical accuracy that is embodied in its pages.

When I became a middle-aged student at a theological college, the lectures I most enjoyed were those concerned with biblical studies. I had had a long career as a theoretical physicist, and the instinct of a scientist in approaching any new field of enquiry is to ask first what are the basic phenomena that will motivate and control the search for a truthful understanding of what is going on. In considering questions of Christian belief, the Bible gives us accounts of the history of Israel, the life, death and resurrection of Jesus, and the first thoughts and experiences of his earliest follow-ers. These are the foundational phenomena of the Christian tradition. I wish to assess them with care and intellectual scrupulosity and so I have endeavoured in this book not to make assertions that do not have significant scholarly sup-port. I have sought only to say things that I believe I could defend with academically respectable argument, even if I do not always set out here all the detail of that argument, often being content simply to indicate its general character. Since the book is angled to the general reader, rather than to the academy, I have not peppered it with scholarly paragraphs and related footnotes that would seek to make good my claim for academic respectability by delving into details of specialist studies. For a similar reason, I have concentrated on trying to illuminate the primary understanding of the text as it stands in the pages of Scripture, rather than moving on to give an account of the extensive theological theorizing that has flowed from that text. In discussing New

Testament issues, for example, my concern is with questions such as the reliability of our knowledge of the historical Jesus and the attitudes of the first generation of Christians, rather than the subsequent history of Christological thinking in the Church. Nevertheless, theological theorizing cannot be wholly absent, and I do comment from time to time about how ancient scriptural insights might relate to modern scientific understandings. But that is not the main burden of the book. Its principal purpose is simply to help the contemporary reader to engage in a serious and intellectually responsible encounter with the Bible.

For those who might want to take the academic issues further, I have added a Further Reading section in which I list a highly selective number of books that I believe might prove useful resources. All my scriptural quotations are taken from the New Revised Standard Version of the Bible. It is the version I mostly use in my own reading, because it seems to me to stick closely to, and to convey well, the sense of the original Greek and Hebrew.

1

Scripture

Ancient pictures of the four evangelists sometimes show them sitting at their desks while a small bird, representing the Holy Spirit, whispers in their ear to tell them what to write. Is that what the Bible is: a divinely dictated book, every word of which conveys absolute and unquestionable truth? I do not think so. For me it is something altogether more subtle. Just as God does not write universal messages in the sky but works more hiddenly, inspiring and guiding individuals and communities, so in a similar way Scripture is inspired by God but written by human beings, in order to be interpreted and understood by them in their succeeding generations. To use an analogy that comes naturally to me as a scientist, the Bible is not the ultimate textbook in which one can look up ready-made answers to all the big questions, but is more like a laboratory notebook, in which are recorded critical historical experiences through which aspects of the divine will and nature have been most accessibly revealed. I believe that the nature of divine revelation is not the mysterious transmission of infallible propositions which are to be accepted without question, but the record of persons and events through which the divine will and nature have been most transparently made known.

Together with their Jewish brothers and sisters, Christians believe that God chose ancient Israel as the people through whose history the divine purpose for all humanity would begin to be most clearly disclosed. It might perhaps seem odd for God to have concentrated on a single nation in this way, and I certainly do not think it means that there was no divine concern for other peoples. In fact, I believe that all the great world faith traditions preserve, in their different manners and in different degrees, genuine accounts of encounter with sacred reality. Yet I believe that God's dealing with Israel had a special significance. This specific focus on Israel reflects an aspect of what it means to speak of God in personal terms, as 'Father' rather than 'Force'. The force of gravity is always the same. It will cause the death of saints and sinners alike if they step off the top of a tall building. Persons are different. They express their personhood by behaving in specific ways in response to specific situations. Of course, personal language about God is being used in some 'stretched' or analogical sense – no one believes that God is an old man with a beard way above the bright blue sky. What this language is seeking to express is the important truth that God is not simply a Being of abstract generality – a universal creative principle, or the God of the philosophers, say – but a God who does particular things with particular people in particular circumstances. The calling of Israel, and the role of particular persons in its history (the individual prophets, for example), reflect this personal style of divine self-disclosure.

This 'scandal of particularity', as it is sometimes called, is even more intensely encountered in the form of a second belief, foundational to Christianity, which asserts the unique significance of Jesus Christ. At the heart of Christian faith lies the mysterious and exciting idea that the infinite and invisible God, beyond finite human powers to conceive adequately, has acted to make the divine nature known in the most fitting and accessible manner possible through the life of a first-century Jew in whom humanity and divinity were both truly present. I shall not stop here to explain why I believe this astonishing claim to be true (it is a task that I have attempted elsewhere; see Further Reading), but it is essential to grasp this belief if we are to understand the proper role that Scripture plays in Christian thinking. The Word of God uttered to humanity is not a written text but a life lived, a painful and shameful death accepted, and the divine faithfulness vindicated through the great act of Christ's resurrection. Scripture contains witness to the incarnate Word, but it is not the Word himself. Its testimony is that 'The Word became flesh and lived among us, and we have seen his glory, the glory as of a father's only Son, full of grace and truth' (John 1.14).

For the Christian, the unique significance of the Bible is that it gives us indispensable accounts of God's acts in Israel and in Jesus Christ. Without that scriptural record we would know little about Israel and very little indeed about Jesus of Nazareth. These events happened in the course of history and the accounts that we have of them necessarily originated at specific times and in particular cultural contexts. Yet the revelatory character claimed for them implies that insights of enduring significance are embedded in the pages of Scripture. A central task for the Christian interpreter of Scripture is to discern what in the Bible has lasting truthful authority, rightly commanding the continuing respect of successive generations, and what is simply time-bound cultural expression, demanding no necessary continuing allegiance from us today. Absolutely no one is free from having to make judgements of this kind. Even the most conservative biblical interpreters are not so single-mindedly fundamentalist as to feel that they must refrain from planting two kinds of seed in the same field or wearing clothes made of two sorts of material (Leviticus 19.19; Deuteronomy 22.9–11). These injunctions are so obviously irrelevant to us today that their abandonment passes essentially unnoticed in the Christian community. At quite the other end of the spectrum is the much more serious and perplexing issue, about which there is a great deal of strongly expressed contemporary disagreement, of what degree of relevance there might be for the Christian today in the clearly expressed prohibition of homosexual sexual intercourse given in Leviticus 18.22. Is this simply a condemnation uttered in a society which saw such activity as wilful perversion and had no possible notion of the modern insight that there is a significant innate element in sexual orientation? Or is it much more than that? The problems that are currently agitating the Anglican Communion on this issue essentially arise from deep-seated differences concerning the nature of Scripture and scriptural authority.

The issue of what is temporary and culturally adventitious in Scripture and what is permanently insightful and authoritative is not confined to the Old Testament. Almost all Christians today treat Paul's emphatic insistence on women covering their heads at worship (1 Corinthians 11.2–16) as no more than a culturally specific way of expressing a degree of dignified respect, in a manner that was appropriate in his particular society but which is not binding on ours. But equally, all Christians will attach abiding significance to the verses that follow (23–26), which give Paul's account of

Christ's institution of Holy Communion at the Last Supper. The problem of discriminating between the time-bound and the permanent is one that will recur throughout this book.

Not all of the Bible is great literature. Some parts are plainly pedestrian and some downright boring (for example, 1 Chronicles 1—8). Yet much of its writing is profound and touches us at very deep levels. In the English-speaking world, the King James Version (AV) contains some of the most moving and best loved passages in our literature. Its cadences have been an influence shaping English literary style over centuries, and many of its characters have powerful archetypal status, even today. Think of the stories of Adam and Eve, Noah, Samson and David. There is an inexhaustibly rich character to all great literature, whose depths are never fully plumbed. There is always the possibility of further meaning awaiting the receptive reader. One of the defects of a self-confident and narrow Biblicism is to ignore this fact by attempting to insist on the single meaning of an allegedly plain text. Such an approach may suit the cookery book, but it will not do for the Bible. Of course, I am not arguing for an 'anything goes' approach to scriptural interpretation, but affirming the expectation that a multilayered over-plus of meaning will often be found in the sacred text. We shall see something of this flexible search for significance when we come later to consider how the New Testament writers made use of the Hebrew Bible, which provided them with their scriptural context. In the early Christian centuries, the Church Fathers often sought to recognize four levels of meaning present in the Bible, essentially the literal, the moral, the symbolic and the spiritual. Sometimes this scheme could lead to strange flights of fanciful interpretation, but in general it was a sound insight to be open to the wealth of significance present in Scripture. The lyrical eroticism of the Song of Songs surely originated in an intense human love affair, but it was not wilful manipulation on the part of the medieval abbot, Bernard of Clairvaux, to reinterpret the Song in terms of the exchange of love between God and the individual human soul. A profound analogy was being identified and explored.

Later in the Middle Ages, and particularly in Reformation times, a more single-meaning approach was pursued in the interpretation of a book then held to be so clear in what it said that whoever runs might read it. Interestingly, this narrowed exegetical stance has been linked with an analogous change in the human attitude to nature. In their bestiaries, the earlier medievals had tended to see the natural world primarily as a source of symbolic representations of spiritual truths. A new concern with natural history for its own sake developed which took a cool and factual look at what was going on, and this is often seen as having been an influence in the eventual development of modern science. There was undoubted gain in being able to recognize the pelican as a bird and not just as a symbol of the Holy Eucharist. However, as centuries later the Romantic Movement was to insist, there is a richness in the natural world that rightly encourages us to find in it too a variety of levels of meaning. There is more to the rainbow than optical theory can express. Something similar is certainly true of the Bible. A much richer and more subtle approach is required than can be accommodated by the concept of a single strand of meaning.

Recognition of the many-layered potentiality of Scripture is vital for a full appropriation of the riches to be found in the Bible. Exploration of the resource that this offers is an on-going process, whose development is spread over succeeding generations. The original meaning intended by the scriptural writer, if it can be discerned, is certainly of significance, but that is not the end of the matter, as we saw with Bernard and the Song. In my final chapter I shall consider a particularly pregnant passage from Paul's letter to the Romans and I shall suggest that it throws helpful light on how we may think theologically about the scientific fact of an evolving universe. Of course, I am not being so absurdly anachronistic as to suppose that Paul had this kind of interpretation in mind, but I do not believe it to be wilful distortion of Scripture for us to use it in this way.

On any particular occasion, the way in which we approach Scripture will be influenced by the sort of questions that we then have in mind. Sometimes the quest will be evidential, as when we are attempting to assess the historical validity of the Hebrew accounts of the Exodus from Egypt, or the gospel accounts of Jesus of Nazareth. Then it is appropriate to be scrupulously concerned with questions such as the identification and reliability of the sources involved and the degree to which the stories have been further developed and elaborated subsequent to the events themselves. In this mode of reading, we are putting Scripture to the test, in a way that is perfectly appropriate. If we believe that God has acted in the history of Israel and in Jesus of Nazareth, it is of primary significance to try to establish as clearly as possible what those actions actually were. The religion of the Incarnation has to take issues of historical truth absolutely seriously. Of course there is a significant power simply in the story itself, but there is an additional power present when it is perceived to be a *true* story. We recognize this frequently in ordinary life. The idea that a somewhat raffish German businessman might risk his life to save the lives of many persecuted Jews is a moving tale. But what gives the story of Oskar Schindler its particular power and poignancy is that he actually was just such a man. One of the most moving moments in the film *Schindler's List* comes at the end, when a long succession of Jews one by one place stones on Schindler's tomb, able to do so because his generous and brave action has actually saved them from an otherwise certain death.

When we are assessing the historical truth to be found in Scripture, we are quite properly subjecting the Bible to critical analysis. However, there is another mode of reading Scripture in which it is the readers themselves who are being put to the test. Great truths are set forth and great hopes are proclaimed. How we respond is of important significance for our lives. We are no longer questioning the Bible, but the Bible is questioning us. Or rather God is questioning us through Scripture. The manner of reading Scripture which medieval monasticism called *lectio divina* – divine reading in which a short passage is meditatively read and reread to allow it to sink into heart and mind – is a prime way in which we can submit ourselves to the power of the Bible.

The earliest parts of the Bible are about three thousand years old and even the most recent are almost two thousand. These writings were composed in cultures very different from that of today, not least because of the great changes in our picture of the world in which we live which have been given us by modern science. We no longer think that we inhabit a three-decker universe. These changes in cultural perspective have to be taken into account in interpreting Scripture, but they by no means imply that the Bible is merely of antiquarian interest. Classic literature, whether that of the Greek tragedians or that of the Hebrew prophets, the Gospel of John or the plays of Shakespeare, has a deep power to speak across the centuries, and it is precisely this ability to break through the confines of locality and epoch which is the authentic sign of great writing. The continuing influence of the Bible on Christian thought and worship witnesses to the profound value of Scripture.

In these few pages I have sought to outline by way of introduction the spirit in which I seek to approach the Bible. The notion of an inerrant text is inappropriately idolatrous, but merely to regard Scripture as an antiquarian deposit that does not need to be taken too seriously today would be an equally grave mistake. Scripture, together with the worshipping experience of the Church and its accumulated traditions of insight, as well as the exercise of our God-given powers of reason, together form the context for Christian thinking and living. As a scientist, I am what I like to call a 'bottom-up thinker', someone who is wary of attempting too much generality before ideas have been sifted and tested against the particularities of experience. The attitude to Scripture which I have tried to sketch needs now to be clarified by attacking a number of specific issues that arise in the course of interpreting the Bible. The chapters that follow will attempt just such an exercise.

2

Development

The sixth chapter of the book of Joshua tells the familiar story of the siege of Jericho, culminating in the collapse of its walls at the blast of the Israelite trumpets, thus enabling the city to be captured. When this passage is set in the Anglican lectionary for reading in church, it ends at verse 20, the moment of the advance of the army into the city, and it omits the verse that follows, which states, 'Then they devoted to destruction by the edge of the sword all in the city, both men and women, young and old, oxen, sheep and donkeys.' These terrible words are certainly ones that a modern reader would find it hard to follow with the proclamation 'This is the word of the Lord'. Yet honesty requires us to acknowledge that tales of massacre and genocide, presented as if these acts were fulfilments of God's will, are not uncommon in the Hebrew Bible. In 1 Samuel 15, Saul is rebuked for not wholeheartedly obeying the command to 'utterly destroy the sinners of the Amalekites, and fight against them till they are consumed' (v. 18), and Samuel tells him that as a result of this disobedience he is rejected from being king over Israel. How can we square this picture of a vengeful God with the one given us by Jesus, who tells us to love our enemies (Matthew 5.43–48)? The simple answer is that we cannot.

I believe that response to this dilemma demands the recognition that the record of revelation contained in Scripture is one of a developing understanding of the divine will and nature, continuously growing over time but never complete, and quite primitive in its earliest stages. Only slowly and falteringly could progress be made in Israel towards gaining a fuller comprehension of the reality of God. The early Israelites had grasped the exclusive nature of the lordship of God, the One whose claims denied the possibility of serving other gods, such as the deities of Canaanite religion. Exodus tells us that the first commandment of the Law given at Sinai proclaimed 'you shall have no other gods before me' (20.3). Ancient Israel went on to interpret this to imply a divine command to destroy the followers of false gods in the Promised Land by a ruthless holy war against them. A primitive society could conceive no better insight than the use of force against unbelievers as the expression of its faithful following of Yahweh, the God of Israel. Yet Scripture also contains the account of a developing and deeper understanding, as God spoke to the Jewish people through the words of the prophets. By the time of the exile in Babylon, the prophet whom we call Second Isaiah had a message very different from that delivered by Samuel to Saul. Particularly significant are the four 'Servant Songs' (Isaiah 42.1–4; 49.1–6; 50.4–9; 52.13—53.12), which speak of a mysterious figure who will play an important role in the fulfilling of the divine purpose. The first of these songs speaks of the Servant as one 'who will not cry or lift up his voice, or make it heard in the street; a bruised reed he will not break, and a dimly burning wick he will not quench' (42.2–3). The Servant is not a powerful military figure, like Joshua or David, winning victory in battle. Nor is he someone who rejects the weak and ineffective, the 'bruised reeds' and the 'dimly burning wicks'. The last two songs speak clearly of a suffering Servant, one who 'gave my back to those who struck me' (50.6) and who was 'wounded for our transgressions, crushed for our iniquities; upon him was the punishment that made us whole, and by his bruises we are healed' (53.5). The Servant brings benefit to all humanity, for he has a saving significance beyond the bounds of Israel alone. God says to him, 'I will give you as a light to the nations, that my salvation may reach to the end of the earth' (49.6). Christians believe that these prophecies found their fulfilment in Jesus, a crucified messiah rather than the hoped-for militant fighter against Roman occupying power.

Clearly very great development had taken place in between Joshua and Second Isaiah, and who can doubt that it had resulted from a deeper and truer understanding of God and God's ways? Accepting this enables us to acknowledge the crudities and atrocities present in early Scripture without being driven to discard belief in the spiritual value of the Bible. We can recognize within it an unfolding process of insight and understanding as God's nature was progressively revealed.

In the earliest strata that scholars can discern in the Hebrew Bible, the belief of Israel is what is sometimes called henotheism. Yahweh is uniquely the One whom Israel worships and to whom it owes exclusive allegiance, but at this stage the deities of the surrounding tribes are treated as having some kind of reality also. Hence the rather strange wording of the first commandment, 'you shall have no other gods *before* [or perhaps, 'besides'] me'. By the time of Second Isaiah, henotheism has uncompromisingly become monotheism. There is no divine reality at all other than Yahweh. 'I am the

Lord, that is my name; my glory I give to no other, nor my praise to idols'. 'Before me no god was formed, nor shall there be any after me' (Isaiah 42.8; 43.10).

Another important development in Hebrew thought related to the nature of individual responsibility. Primitive society tended to think in collective terms, with the family spread out over successive generations as the primary unit. Hence the second commandment can speak of God as 'a jealous God, punishing children for the iniquity of parents, to the third and the fourth generation of those who reject me' (Exodus 20.5). When Achan is convicted of stealing forbidden booty, his whole family is stoned and burnt with him (Joshua 7.22–26). By the time of the exilic prophet Ezekiel, an individualized understanding had replaced this terrible way of thinking which condemned the innocent with the guilty. 'The person who sins shall die. A child shall not suffer for the iniquity of a parent, nor a parent for the iniquity of a child' (Ezekiel 18.20; see also Jeremiah 31.30). The multilayered structure of the book of Deuteronomy (5.9 and 24.16) expresses both these points of view.

This developmental perspective on Scripture also helps to explain many of the apparent contradictions present in its pages. Often passages in the canonical text, presented as if they were a unity, have in fact been formed by intermingling material drawn from a variety of sources, composed at different times and, therefore, reflecting different stages of development. In Israel there was a continual reworking of key narratives, a task which extended over centuries. The process of identifying and dating the sources involved is a matter of scholarly activity and debate. The details of the arguments involved need not concern us here, but even the careful reader of an English translation will often be aware of the issues. A simple example, to which we shall give more detailed attention in the chapter that follows, is provided by the creation accounts in the first two chapters of Genesis. The account that stands first in Scripture (1.1—2.3), but which is certainly the later of the two, is of considerable sophistication and consistently uses a single Hebrew word for God (*elohim*) to refer to the Creator. The second account (2.4–25) is more primitive and refers to the Creator as the Lord God, the first word of this title being the English translation of the Hebrew *Yahweh*, the proper name of God, which was considered to be so holy that a pious Jew could not utter it aloud but instead said the word *adonai*, meaning Lord. In a literal-minded way of reading them, the two accounts are incompatible. For example, in the first the creation of humans follows the creation of the animals, while in the second the order is reversed. Even greater confusion is present in the story of the Flood. In the opening verses, God tells Noah to take a pair of each of all the animals into the Ark (Genesis 6.19), but later God's instruction is to take seven pairs of all clean animals, but only one pair of unclean animals (Genesis 7.2). Here again, at least two different sources have been combined, with the second exhibiting a priestly concern about issues of ritual cleanness and uncleanness.

Another example of the multilayered character of Scripture is provided by the way in which Deuteronomy gives its own account of the story of the Exodus, together with significant amplifications of the Law as it is presented in the books Exodus and Leviticus. Leviticus itself very clearly illustrates the way in which there was often a cumulative process of editing and reworking, stretching over a long period of time. A great deal of the book is taken up with immensely detailed regulations about various types of sacrifice and the specification of how the Aaronic priesthood was to be organized in order to offer them. These rules are presented as if they were proclaimed by Moses to apply to the worship of the Tabernacle, the sacred tent accompanying the Israelites in their desert wanderings. While there may well have been such a tent, it is surely clear that these complex and detailed regulations must largely refer to the settled worship of the Jerusalem Temple. The final form of Leviticus is likely to have originated in priestly circles about the time of the return from exile and the rebuilding of the Temple which had been destroyed by Nebuchadnezzar.

Thus it is clear that before the Hebrew Bible reached its final canonical form there was a long developmental process, involving reworking of much that had been inherited from the past in the light of the understanding and experience of the present. Yet the editors who assembled the final text apparently did not find it necessary to smooth out the differences present in the sources that they used. Instead, the deposit of many generations was often allowed to stand together in the formation of Scripture. The long process of development was not obliterated in order to produce the appearance of a single consistent text. The explorations of the past were not to be totally obscured from view.

The Old Testament contains material spanning perhaps a thousand years, but the New Testament is much more temporally compact. I believe that all, or almost all, of its books were written before the end of the first century. Probably the earliest Christian writing available to us is Paul's first letter to the Thessalonians, composed about the year 50. (The crucifixion was in either 30 or 33.) There would have been a preceding period of oral transmission in a culture where this skill was commonly and carefully exercised, and possibly there were some early written sources now lost to us. Scholars argue about this latter possibility because of the striking verbal similarities evident in some of the material incorporated into both Matthew and Luke. They think this may have arisen from the fact that both evangelists used a written source no longer extant, which academics call Q (from the German *Quelle*, source). There is also a good deal of agreement that the texts that we have preserve within them some formulations of the beliefs of early Christians which had originated even closer to the events themselves. An example would be the confession 'Jesus is Lord' (see Romans 10.9), which seems to have been a very early statement of Christian belief.

The first century was a time of great theological ferment and creativity in the Christian Church, as it strove to articulate and interpret its experience of the new transforming grace that it believed had come to it from its risen Lord, Jesus Christ. We shall have to give this more consideration later. The richness and variety of the theological insight that arose from this engagement with experience is clearly expressed in the pages of the New Testament. It is significant that the Church preserved the multiple perspectives offered by the four Gospels, rather than attempting a conflated harmonization. It was soon recognized that the Gospel of John had a different character from the other three. Clement of Alexandria (second century) was to call it a 'spiritual gospel'. The Gospel is certainly bold in its assertion of the divine character of Christ, but it is also the Gospel that shows the greatest concern for the dating and location of the events it describes. Despite the timeless character of many of the statements made in it, John's account is anchored in events in first-century Palestine.

Perhaps the strangest book of the New Testament is the Revelation of John. In fact, because of this it had some difficulty in gaining a place in the canon. Its author seems to have had some connection with the community of the author of the fourth Gospel, but a comparison of their respective styles of writing, plainly discernible in English translation, shows that they were certainly not the same person. Revelation illustrates the mixed character of Scripture as hope and horror mingle in its pages. There are deeply moving pictures of the worship of heaven (ch. 4 etc.). There is a profoundly hopeful conclusion (21.1—22.7). But there are also terrifyingly brutal descriptions of divinely inflicted punishment (the sequences of seals, trumpets and plagues in chapters 6—10 and 16), presented as manifestations of the wrath of God. The failure of subsequent generations to recognize that these apocalyptic images of divine vengeance arose in the particular context of a time of intense persecution, and that they should be evaluated as human responses to that situation rather than as unalterable expressions of the timeless divine will, has had a baleful influence on much subsequent Christian thinking. No book of the New Testament has been more unfortunate in its interpretation and influence than Revelation.

The unfolding process of developing theological understanding that we find in the Bible has continued beyond the confines of Scripture itself. The fundamental experiences and insights of the New Testament period led eventually to the Christological and Trinitarian conclusions of the Church Councils of the fourth and fifth centuries. The Councils' understandings arose from engaging with the testimony of the Bible, for example from the way in which the New Testament writers – despite being monotheistic Jews who knew he had recently lived a human life – seemed driven to use divine-sounding words about their experience of the risen Christ, thereby producing an obvious tension that is unresolved in the New Testament itself. The later theological theories of the Councils derived from the New Testament witness, but their details are not clearly articulated in its pages. And, of course, these Councils did not mark the end of theological development. The Fathers had sought to draw the boundaries within which they believed orthodox Christian thinking needed to be contained if it were to be a true witness, but there has remained a need for further exploration and reflection. Those who believe in the continuing work of the Holy Spirit (John 16.13) will not find this surprising. The role of development, within Scripture and after it, depends upon the fact that revelational disclosure is primarily personal rather than propositional, living and not petrified.

3

Creation and Fall

————•◦•————

Often when the relation between science and the Bible is under discussion it is the opening chapters of Genesis that are the focus of attention. Read in a flat-footedly literal way they are obviously incompatible with the well-founded conclusions of modern cosmology and evolutionary biology. We have very good reasons to believe that the universe is 13.7 billion years old; that initially it was an almost uniform expanding ball of energy which gradually, under the condensing effect of gravity, became lumpy with stars and galaxies; that in the first generation of these stars, processes in their internal nuclear furnaces enriched the chemical potentiality of the universe, adding many heavier elements to the hydrogen and helium that were its aboriginal constituents, thereby enabling the possibility of an eventual development of carbon-based life; that on our planet this possibility was realized, at first in the form of single-celled organisms; and that eventually life became progressively more complex through biological evolution until conscious animals and self-conscious hominids emerged as astonishing examples of the rich potentiality that had been present in that initial ball of energy.

This remarkable history of creative fertility is, of course, very different in form from that of the two stories told in chapters 1 and 2 of Genesis. We have already seen that the fact that these two stories themselves are incompatible with each other should warn us against treating them as if they were divinely dictated accounts, given to save us the trouble of scientific investigation into terrestrial and cosmic history. In reading any form of literature, part of the respect that we show it is to be careful to identify the genre of what is before us. Different kinds of writing have to be understood in different kinds of ways. Poetry is very different from prose. When the poet Robert Burns tells us that his love 'is like a red, red rose', we know that he is not asserting that his girlfriend has green leaves and prickles! The Bible is not really a book but a library. It has within it a variety of different genres: poetry, prose, story, history, laws, letters, and so on. Part of a proper respect for Scripture is to be aware of this issue of genre. The sad irony of so-called 'creationism', based on a fundamentalist biblical literalism, is that in fact it abuses the very text that it seeks to respect, missing the point of what is written by mistaking its genre. For example, Genesis 1 does not give us a quasi-scientific account of a hectic six days of divine activity, but is something altogether deeper and more interesting than that. It is a theological text whose principal purpose is to assert that nothing exists except through the will of God. Eight times we are told 'And God said let there be . . .' and that what was divinely spoken then came to pass.

In fact, from the earliest Christian centuries it was recognized that Genesis is not giving a literal account. People noted that light was created on the first day but the sun, moon and stars, the apparent sources of light, only appeared on the fourth day. The Church Fathers, such as Augustine and Gregory of Nyssa, understood that the 'days' of creation could not be literal periods of 24 hours and some considered that they might stand for vast expanses of time. In fact, the late creation of the heavenly bodies in the narrative illustrates the theological character of Genesis 1. In the ancient world, sun, moon and stars were often worshipped as deities. Genesis is at pains to make it clear that they are merely creatures, appearing rather late on the scene in order to indicate their properly subordinate status. That is why Genesis does not use the proper names, Sun and Moon, which were also the names of pagan deities, but refers simply to the greater and the lesser lights.

The much older story of Genesis 2 is even more obviously mythical in its character, meaning by 'myth' not a fairy story but a truth so deep that only story can convey it. This second chapter of Genesis offers important theological insights by means of the story that it tells: humanity's place within nature, as God forms Adam from the dust of the earth; the presence, nevertheless, of a transcendent dimension in human life as God inspires Adam with the breath of life; human responsibility for the care of nature, conveyed in the image of tilling a garden; an intimate connection between men and women, conveyed (albeit with some patriarchal overtones) in the story of the creation of Eve from Adam's rib, and also asserting their essential equality and unity as 'one flesh'.

The account of Genesis 1 was written either during the Exile or shortly thereafter. Many scholars believe that it was influenced by encounter with Babylonian creation myths. No doubt there is some truth in this, but a comparison of Genesis 1 with the Babylonian myth *Enuma Elish* reveals some striking differences. In the latter, Marduk, the god of Babylon, fights and slays Tiamath, the great sea monster, slicing her dead body in half to form earth and sky out of the two pieces. Fortunately, no such story, deeply embarrassing to a modern reader, is to be found in Genesis. Instead its account, though certainly not the same as that given by modern science and inevitably expressed in the idioms of its day, is nevertheless astonishingly 'sensible' from a modern point of view. Creation is portrayed as a process (the six days); it begins with a kind of burst of energy ('Let there be light'); although all happens at God's bidding, nature has its own part to play ('Let the earth bring forth . . .', vv. 11, 20, 24); the sequence is plants, sea creatures and birds, land animals, human beings. This ordering is not perfect – the birds come too early and the plants arrive before the sun is there to fuel photosynthesis – but it is an astonishing improvement on Marduk and Tiamath. I am not attempting to claim an anachronistic consonance between the Bible and modern science, but overall Genesis is remarkably less embarrassing than the *Enuma Elish* would be if it were part of Scripture.

Another important difference between Babylonian and Hebrew thinking relates to the status of humanity. In the former's account, human beings were created simply to be the slaves of the gods, but in Genesis 1.28 human beings are deputed to be divine representatives in the governance of nature. This is linked with the celebrated statement that humanity is created 'in the image of God' (v. 27). Some scholars have seen here an echo of the ancient imperial practice of erecting statues of the Emperor in distant provinces of his dominion as signs and reminders of his authority. Be that as it may, surely the language of the image of God has also a deeper reference than that. Over the centuries, many have seen the unique human capacity for rational thinking as forming the core of the divine image. However, I doubt whether this really gets to the heart of the matter. Surely that image is to be found in the mentally handicapped as well as in the academically brilliant. Its presence is the theological basis for a fundamental belief in the worth of every individual human being. To my mind, it is the love of God bestowed on each individual, and the implicit ability to be aware of the divine presence, that constitute the essence of the *imago dei*.

While so much discussion of science and the Bible has focussed on Genesis, it is important to recognize that there are many other parts of Scripture that refer to God's creation. Many of them are to be found in the wisdom writings, which form a distinct strand in the Hebrew Bible. The sages see things differently from the way of the priests and prophets. The latter appeal repeatedly to the revelatory events of salvation history, such as the great deliverance from slavery accomplished in the Exodus from Egypt. The sages see revelation in more general terms. They look at what is regularly going on in the world, clearly perceived and candidly evaluated. Their pragmatism means that they often seem worldly wise in their judgements. 'Take the garment of one who has given surety for a stranger; seize the pledge given as surety for foreigners' (Proverbs 27.13). Their more theological reflections often centre on a personified figure of Wisdom, seen as God's consort in the creation of the world (Proverbs 8.22–31). Their cool gaze takes in the natural world. 'Three things are too wonderful for me; four I do not understand: the way of an eagle in the sky, the way of a snake on a rock, the way of a ship on the high seas, and the way of a man with a girl' (Proverbs 30.18–19; see also the following verses, 21–31). The wisdom writers are the nearest that ancient Israel got to anything remotely like a dispassionate scientific attitude.

Anyone who is looking for scriptural resources for a service on the theme of science and religion will find much more material in the Old Testament than in the New, and it is from the wisdom writers that much of this material will come.

In addition, some of the psalms also contain important references to nature. For example, Psalm 104 is a paean of praise to God for the rich wonder of creation. 'O LORD, how manifold are your works, in wisdom you have made them all' (v. 24). The steady gaze of the psalmist takes in things as they actually are, not hesitating to declare that 'The young lions roar for their prey, seeking their food from God' (v. 21). The whole panorama of nature is surveyed, with human beings only mentioned in three of the 32 verses. The great nineteenth-century physicist, James Clerk Maxwell, who was a devout Christian, had the second verse of Psalm 111, 'Great are the works of the Lord, studied by all who delight in them', inscribed in Latin on the entrance gates into the Cavendish Laboratory in Cambridge.

The greatest of all the wisdom writings is surely the book of Job, a profound tale of human suffering. For 37 chapters, calamities fall on Job and he and his friends argue about the significance of the terrible things that have happened to him and his family. The friends assert that he must have offended God by his sins and so he is receiving just punishment. Job protests his innocence and longs to be able to appear directly before God to mount his defence and make his just protest. Then, suddenly, God is there. 'The LORD answered Job out of the whirlwind' (Job 38.1). This divine response is quite extraordinary. Instead of dealing with the origin of the poor man's plight (presented in an older prose prologue to the main poetical text of the book as having arisen from a highly questionable wager in the heavenly court between God and Satan), the Lord simply takes Job on a tour of the wonders of creation, including contemplating the hippopotamus and the crocodile, described in exalted mythical terms (Job 38—41). At one point (40.15) the Lord says 'Look at Behemoth [the apotheosized hippopotamus, treated as a symbol of the non-human creation], which I made just as I made you'. The point seems to be that the Creator values and cares for all creatures in appropriate ways. All of nature is part of the great drama of creation, and it is not there just to be a backdrop to the human play. Apparently this encounter with the Lord, and the display of divine creative majesty, is enough for Job, even after all his suffering. He replies, 'I had heard of you by the hearing of the ear, but now my eye sees you; therefore I despise myself and repent in dust and ashes' (Job 42.5–6). The whole of nature is to be seen as a theophany, a revelation of the Creator.

This value of all creation in the eyes of its Creator is affirmed in a striking way in the New Testament. In a remarkable Christological hymn in Colossians (1.15–20), it is proclaimed that Christ 'reconciles all *things* [not just all people] by the blood of his cross' (v. 20). This is a theme to which we shall return briefly in the final chapter.

The wisdom writers were what we might today call 'natural theologians'. That is to say, they were seeking to learn something of God through general experience, without overt appeal to the particularities of specific revelatory events. While this approach is valid, it has its limitations. Its appeal to limited forms of experience can only yield limited insight. Perhaps this explains why, in the later wisdom writings such as Ecclesiastes, one finds a degree of reserve about attainable human understanding: 'Who knows whether the spirit of man goes upward and the spirit of the beast goes down to the earth?' (Ecclesiastes 3.21).

Returning to the opening chapters of Genesis, it is time to look at chapter 3, the story of the Fall. Once again we have to recognize that we are dealing with the genre of myth. I do not believe that the chapter is the historical account of a single disastrous ancestral act, but it is a story conveying truth about the relationship between God and humanity. Read in a literal way, the story would clearly be incompatible with well-established knowledge given us by the scientific study of the past. Snakes do not speak, thorns and thistles did not arise as a result of an act of human disobedience and, most important of all, death was present in the world long before it had any hominid inhabitants. After all, it was the extinction of the dinosaurs, about 65 million years ago, that gave the little furry mammals, who are our genetic ancestors, their evolutionary opportunity. Any attempt to struggle with these difficulties in order to try to find a literal interpretation of the chapter is, in fact, once again to miss the point. Once the story's mythic power is released from bondage to a fundamentalist reading, it becomes full of insight of a kind that can be seen as complementary to the insights afforded us by science. I believe that the story of the Fall should be interpreted in the following manner.

Human beings are self-conscious in a way that I believe greatly exceeds any animal experience of consciousness, even in the case of the higher primates who are our nearest evolutionary cousins. By self-consciousness I mean not just a degree of heightened self-awareness, but also the remarkable human power to project our thoughts far into the future and back into the past. I believe that the primates simply live in what one may call the near present. The chimpanzee can figure out that if he throws up the stick, the banana may fall down, but he does not sit there brooding on the fact that in ten or twenty years' time he will be dead. Human beings, on the contrary, do live aware that they will die, even when that event is likely to be many years away. It is almost impossible to imagine the dawning of this self-conscious power, or to know where along the chain of hominid evolution it first emerged. Nevertheless, it is certain that it happened. Presumably, it was not a single discrete event in which our ancestors suddenly realized that they could use the future tense, but a gradual process. I believe that this process will have been accompanied by a dawning consciousness of the presence of God (the formation of the *imago dei*), a capacity that I do not think the animals possess. In the course of this process of the correlated emergence of these distinctive hominid powers of perception, there was a turning of our ancestors away from the pole of God and into the pole of the human self. That process, of which we are still the heirs, was the Fall. In the powerful imagery of Genesis 3, the serpent tempts Eve to eat the forbidden fruit by whispering in her ear the promise that if she does so 'your eyes will be opened and you will be like God, knowing good and evil' (v. 5). Yet, the promise that she can become her own god is false. The Fall is indeed a fall 'upward', the gaining of knowledge, but it is an error to suppose that humans can thereby attain equality with their Creator, so that they can then live their lives independently of God. This declaration of complete human autonomy, the assertion that we can simply 'do it my way', is the root meaning of sin. The refusal to acknowledge that we are creatures in need of the grace of our Creator is the source of subsequent human sins, those deeds of selfishness and deceit that mar our lives as the result of believing the false claim to be completely independent of the assistance of divine grace.

This turning from God did not bring biological death into the world, for that had been there for many millions of years before there were any hominids. What it did bring was what we may call 'mortality', human sadness and bitterness at the inevitability of death and decay. Because our ancestors had become self-conscious, they knew long beforehand that they were going to die. Because they had alienated themselves from the God whose steadfast faithfulness is the only (and sufficient) true ground for the hope of a destiny beyond death, this realization brought deep sorrow at the transience of human life. Such an understanding brings theological illumination to the interpretation of chapter 5 of Paul's Epistle to the Romans, in which the apostle compares Adam (surely to be understood by us, if not by Paul himself, as a collective symbol for humanity) with Christ. Paul says that 'Just as sin came into the world through one man, and death [mortality] through sin, and so death spread to all because all have sinned' (v. 12), so 'much more surely has the grace of one man, Jesus Christ, abounded for many' (v. 15). Alienation from God brought the bitterness of mortality, but the relation of humanity to God has been restored in the atonement (at-one-ment) brought by Jesus Christ, in whom the life of humanity and the life of divinity are both present and the broken link is mended.

This approach to the Fall illustrates the continuing power of Scripture, persisting under changes of interpretation induced by changes in knowledge and experience. The ancient myth of Adam and Eve in the garden was used by Paul to illuminate the Christian experience of the saving power of Christ, and it can be reinterpreted by us for the same purpose in the light of modern scientific knowledge, in a way that I believe preserves the essential core of its meaning. There is certainly a clear difference in the details of how Paul and we understand the story, but its essential point remains the same. The modern interpretation does, however, exclude one use of the story of the Fall that was frequently made in the early Christian centuries. The perplexing presence of disease and disaster in a creation emphatically declared 'good' in Genesis 1 (vv. 10, 12, 18, 21, 25, 31), was understood by some of the Fathers as being due to the cursing of the ground following human sinful disobedience, which had resulted in the marring of what had originally been a perfect creation. In particular, the supposed entry of death into the world following Adam's transgression could be seen as an example of this. This strategy for explaining the apparent imperfection of a world that is the creation of a perfect Creator is not available to us. Instead, in Chapter 10, we shall take a different approach to the problem of evil and suffering, one that will also be seen to have a relation to the insights of Scripture.

The discussion of this chapter will serve, I hope, to illustrate how ancient religious wisdom and modern scientific knowledge can blend in a way that does justice to the valid insights of both. This is possible because Scripture is not a dead deposit of unchanging meaning, the repository of assertions that have to be accepted at face value without question, but a living spring from which new truths and insight can be expected to continue to flow.

4

Ambiguity

The tapestry of life is not coloured in simple black and white, representing an unambiguous choice between the unequivocally bad and the unequivocally good. The ambiguity of human deeds and desires means that life includes many shades of grey. What is true of life in general is true also of the Bible in particular. An honest reading of Scripture will acknowledge the presence in its pages of various kinds of ambiguity.

We might begin our consideration with the chilling story of Genesis 22, the testing of Abraham by God as the patriarch is told to sacrifice his only son Isaac on Mount Moriah. The narrative tells us that as father and son trudge alone towards the mountain on their solemn journey, the young boy asks, 'Where is the lamb for the burnt offering?' and the father, through gritted teeth we may suppose, replies, 'God himself will provide' (vv. 7–8). It is a moment of great pathos. Why is Abraham, who has repeatedly been promised that his offspring will multiply and become a great nation that will be a blessing to all people, apparently cruelly called upon to sacrifice his beloved only son? Of course, in the end this does not happen and a ram is sacrificed in Isaac's place, but the suffering of the boy and his father in the course of this awful testing seems extraordinarily severe. No doubt, part of the purpose of the story was to make it clear to Israel that child sacrifice, a common practice among the surrounding nations, was not in accordance with the will of God, but this seems such a strange and bitter way in which to make the point. In Christian thinking, the *akedah*, the binding of Isaac as Jewish people call the story, came to be seen as a type (that is to say, a symbolically anticipatory event) of the death on the cross of Jesus the Son of God in obedience to his Father's will. In stained-glass windows portraying the history of salvation, the two events are often represented in close association. Both images reflect the ambiguity of a world in which there is both beauty and ugliness, fruitfulness and wastefulness, joy and sorrow. The Bible does not seek to disguise this fact by an attempt at a facile piety that closes its eyes to the ambiguous strangeness of creation. The problems of evil and suffering are surely the ones that most perplex and trouble the believer. For the Christian, the cross provides a deep and essential insight into this mystery. It is the Son of God who hangs there in the darkness of Golgotha and who utters the paradoxical cry, 'My God, my God, why have you forsaken me?' (Matthew 27.46; Mark 15.34). The Christian God is not simply a compassionate spectator looking down from the invulnerability of heaven onto the strange bitterness of creation but, in the incarnate Christ, is seen as a fellow sufferer in the travail of the world. We shall come back later to the problems of theodicy (the justification of the observed ways of God).

The patriarch Abraham is one of the great figures in religious history. Three world faith traditions, Judaism, Christianity and Islam, look back to him as a person of foundational significance. Yet Abraham is not portrayed as morally flawless. Although he is an archetype of the man who puts his faith in God, Abraham's trust wavers at times. He cannot wait for the fulfilment of the promise of a son in his old age, but fathers Ishmael by his Egyptian slave-girl Hagar (Genesis 16.1–6). When he fears that he is to be killed by Abimelech because the king wants to have Sarah as his wife, Abraham deceitfully pretends that she is his sister (Genesis 20).

Abraham's grandson Jacob, the patriarch of the twelve tribes of Israel, is a man of cunning who swindles his brother Esau out of his birthright and deceives his father Isaac in order to be blessed in the place of his brother (Genesis 25.29–34; 27.1–40). And so the tale of ambiguous character continues. One further example must suffice.

David is an iconic figure in Israelite thought and his kingdom is repeatedly cited as having been a golden age to which later generations of Jews long to return. Yet he too is a person of great moral ambiguity. Not only is there the well-known story of his adultery with Bathsheba and the treacherous murder of her husband Uriah the Hittite (2 Samuel 11), but there is also an ugly incident at the end of David's life. Shimei, a member of the family of Saul, cursed him when he fled from the rebellion raised by his son Absalom. When the rebellion has been put down and David returns, he pardons Shimei in an apparent act of clemency. Yet the insult clearly continues to rankle and on his deathbed David summons his son Solomon, who is to succeed him as king, and urges him to execute Shimei as soon as possible (1 Kings 2.5–9). It is the vengeful act of a spiteful old man.

A quite different kind of ambiguity is represented by the frequent references to angels that appear in both the Old Testament and the New. In both Hebrew and Greek the word translated in English as 'angel' is the simply the common word for a messenger. There are therefore different options for understanding these passages. Does 'angel' refer to a heavenly messenger, a purely spiritual being sent by God? Does it just refer to a human messenger? Is the image of an angelic messenger being used to signify by personification, in a symbolic manner that would be natural in the ancient world, the divinely bestowed gift of an enlightening insight? Different passages may well be interpreted in these different ways, and different people will make different judgements about which interpretation is appropriate.

A somewhat related ambiguity relates to how one should understand some of the biblical miracle stories. I shall later defend my belief that many of the New Testament miracle stories, such as those of Jesus' many healings and the paramount Christian miracle of the Resurrection, are indeed grounded in historical occurrences. However, is that necessarily true of all these stories? Consider, for example, the celebrated miracle story of the turning of water into wine at Cana of Galilee (John 2.1–11). Read as a plain text it might seem to be the account of an almost ludicrous over-reaction to a comparatively mild social embarrassment. The wine may indeed have run out at the wedding feast, but no doubt the guests had already received a pretty reasonable degree of refreshment. Was not the miraculous creation of about 150 gallons of new wine rather excessive? Yet the story is clearly intended to carry a deeper significance beneath its surface meaning. John calls it a 'sign' and at this level it serves to show that the presence of Jesus has a transforming power comparable to the replacement of insipid water by joyful wine. The symbolic charge of the story seems hinted at by the water being contained in six stone jars 'for the Jewish rites of purification'. Is this an indication that the essential message is that in Christ the ritual of Jewish law is replaced by the freedom of the gospel? And does not that imply that the story might simply be a symbolic narrative incorporated into the Gospel as if it were an enacted event? Different interpreters will give different answers to these questions, but that possibility indicates the presence of ambiguity.

Yet another kind of ambiguity appears in the Gospels, an ambiguity not of character but of circumstances. Life is such that there is often no single ideal choice to be made, but all possible actions have an inescapable shadow side of one kind or another. The decision to be made is not the unambiguous choice between black and white, but the much more difficult matter of the selection of the least dark shade of grey. Jesus, living a truly human life, was not exempt from having to make this kind of perplexing decision. In the course of his hectic public ministry, his mother and brothers came to see him. Perhaps they were anxious about the dangerous notoriety he was acquiring and hoped that they could persuade him to return to a quieter and safer life at home. Jesus must have been fully aware of the ties of family responsibility and affection that are so important to Jewish people, but he also knew that his allegiance had to be elsewhere, in fulfilling the will of his heavenly Father. Consequently he treated his family with painful coolness, doubtless because they were seeking to constrain what they saw as his dangerous ministry (Mark 3.21). When he is told that they are outside asking for him, he simply says, 'Who are my mother and my brothers? . . . Whoever does the will of God is my brother and sister and mother' (Mark 3.33–35).

On another occasion, Jesus is in the gentile region of Tyre (Matthew 15.21–28). Perhaps he is seeking an interval of rest from his demanding ministry. Certainly, he does not wish his presence there to be known. Jesus feels that his ministry must be concentrated on 'the lost sheep of Israel', but a gentile woman, whose daughter is ill, seeks him out and clamours for his help. At first Jesus is unwilling. He gives her the harsh-sounding reply, 'It is not fair to take the children's food and throw it to the dogs.' The woman makes the witty response, 'Yes, Lord, but even the dogs eat the crumbs that fall from their master's table.' Jesus is persuaded and her daughter is healed. At first sight, this seems a troubling story about the one whose life was so full of compassionate reaction to the needs of others. I believe that Jesus was wrestling with the ambiguous choice between necessary rest and further healing ministry, together with the need to focus his activity on the Jewish people to whom he had been sent. In his humanity, he was willing to accept the help that the woman's bold response gave him in deciding what he should do.

We have earlier devoted some attention to what is perhaps the greatest ambiguity in Scripture: the stories of conflict and violence that are to be found in its pages. Though most of these are to be found in the Old Testament, a similar note is not wholly absent from the pages of the New. In addition to the violent symbolic language deployed in Revelation, there are also some disturbing incidents to be found elsewhere. One is the story of Ananias and Sapphira (Acts 5.1–11). This couple sell the property that they possess and pretend to give the whole of the proceeds to support the common life of the Jerusalem Church, while actually withholding some of the money for their private use. Peter discerns this and condign divine punishment descends upon the couple, who are successively struck dead as they attempt to lie to Peter. They certainly behaved dishonestly, but their terrible punishment seems disproportionately severe.

A particular kind of ambiguity is presented by the figure of Judas Iscariot, chosen by Jesus to be one of the Twelve, but the disciple who eventually betrayed him to the hostile authorities. Much Christian thinking has seen Judas as wholly evil from the start, as if he were a kind of devil incarnate. I do not think that this is credible in the light of his having been chosen by Jesus. I find helpful the interpretation of Judas offered by Dorothy Sayers in her play-cycle about Jesus, *The Man Born to be King.* She suggests that Judas, like Peter, found it difficult to accept that Jesus was not going to be a militant Messiah who would destroy the forces of the Roman occupying power, but that he was to be a crucified Messiah, accepting the way of suffering (Mark 8.31–33). While Peter was eventually led to accept this, Judas could not. Sayers suggests that he was complicit in handing Jesus over to the authorities because he hoped this would force his Master's hand and compel him to call on a 'legion of angels' (Matthew 26.53) to defeat the Romans. Once he became aware of his tragic mistake, Judas was driven to remorseful despair and suicide.

Outside the Gospels we also encounter the general ambiguity of imperfect humanity. Paul is an example. In his letter to the Romans he is movingly frank about the moral struggle, telling them, 'So I find it to be a law that when I want to do what is good, evil lies close at hand. . . . Wretched man that I am! Who will rescue me from this body of death? Thanks be to God through Jesus Christ our Lord!' (Romans 7.21, 24–25). Paul is often manifestly vulnerable in his need for appreciation and the acknowledgement of his apostolic authority. In his second letter to the Corinthians, pleas for recognition alternate with statements of sublime theological insight: 'Are we beginning to commend ourselves again? Surely we do not need, as some do, letters of recommendation to you or from you, do we?' (2 Corinthians 3.1); 'Now the Lord is the Spirit, and where the Spirit of the Lord is, there is freedom' (3.17). Such ambiguity has, of course, continued in the Church to this day.

5

Israel's Bible

The Hebrew scriptures, which the Christian Church calls the Old Testament, were the Bible of Israel. We have seen already that within them myth, properly understood as deep truth conveyed in the form of symbolic story, has an important role. But so does history, the account of actual happenings. If God chose to reveal the divine nature through a particular relationship with a chosen nation, then gaining knowledge of the actual history of that people must be of considerable importance. Scripture is more than a symbolic story-book.

The identification and evaluation of the historical content of the Hebrew scriptures is a complex matter involving much learned scholarly debate. Moreover, the world of scholarship is not immune from its own version of the tides of fashion. Currently there is a tendency to place great emphasis on the role of the editorial formation of the Hebrew canon in the post-exilic period of Persian influence, when the Jews had returned from Babylon. We believe this to be the time when the Hebrew Bible was compiled in its present final form. Of course, this editorial process must have been important, but I find it difficult not to believe that the editors were working with much material that had originated centuries earlier in Israelite history, providing a record of events that they needed to treat with great seriousness and respect. It seems to me that there is a good deal of evidence of such material still visible in the final form of the text.

As an example, consider Genesis 14, an account of an ancient battle of four kings against five. Abraham becomes involved in the aftermath of the fight because of the capture of his nephew Lot, and he then encounters the mysterious King Melchizedek of Salem, who will eventually provide the unknown author of the Epistle to the Hebrews with a powerful symbol of Christ (Hebrews 5 and 7). This chapter of Genesis is a nightmare to read in church because of the strange names of the ancient Canaanite kings (Chedorlaomer etc.) that are preserved in it. Surely the origin of this chapter, with its wealth of personal identification, must lie in a very ancient text.

For another example, consider the book of Judges, with its account of happenings in Israel after the death of Joshua and before the later formation of the Kingdom under Saul, and then under David. The book has a formulaic structure in which periods of fierce engagements with neighbouring tribes who for a while threaten Israel, are followed by forty-year periods of calm in which 'the land had rest'. There is a primitive savagery about these stories – for example Jael's murder of Sisera (ch. 4), the bloody tale of Abimelech (ch. 9), Jephthah's rash vow that leads to the sacrifice of his daughter (ch. 11), and the highly ambiguous figure of the swaggering strong-man Samson (chs 13—16) – which accords well with these stories originating in the events of a turbulent archaic society, rather than being made up in a later period of calm reflection.

A rather different example is provided by the 'succession narrative' of 2 Samuel 13—1 Kings 2, with its fascinating account of the rebellion of Absalom and the subsequent intrigue and counter-intrigue at the court of the ageing King David, which eventually led to the establishment of his son Solomon as the next ruler of Israel. This story of political machinations has about it an authenticity of detail that persuades me that it is essentially a contemporary account of the rivalry for the throne, giving us a realistic piece of political historical writing originating five centuries before Herodotus.

Of course, in the case of archetypical events such as the Exodus from Egypt, the task of sifting historical fact from later elaboration and legendary accretion is much more tricky and difficult, because of continuing reworking and reflection on these foundational themes. Yet I cannot believe that these accounts are mere confabulations. Rather it must surely be the case that there is a historical deposit contained in them, even if its detail has been developed and extended. Once again we find that different elements are allowed to stand side by side without the final editors succumbing to the temptation to produce a smoothed-out harmonization. It is interesting that in Exodus 14, where the Lord commands Moses to stretch out his hand to part the waters of the Red Sea, the result is apparently achieved by natural means as 'the LORD drove the sea back by a strong east wind all night' (v. 21). The materials scientist Colin Humphreys has given an interesting discussion of how the 'miracles' of Exodus might all have natural explanations, even if their timing would still be seen as providentially significant. As part of his argument the 'Red Sea' is understood to have been a wide marsh, the 'Reed Sea' (which is what the Hebrew phrase used actually means). Humphreys also identifies the dramatic events at Mount Sinai (Exodus 10.18–19) as being a volcanic eruption in north Arabia, rather than taking place at the traditional site of the Holy Mountain.

In evaluating such evidence as can be gleaned from the attitudes to Israel recorded in other Ancient Near Eastern chronicles and then using this in an attempt to provide checks on the historicity of the Hebrew Bible, we need to remember that the latter was written from the standpoint of Israel, for whom Solomon was a great king with a court of cosmopolitan splendour, while from the general standpoint of the ancient world, Israel must have been seen simply as a small state sandwiched between the really great nations of Egypt, Assyria and Babylon, the players of true importance on the international stage. Events in Israelite history need not be expected necessarily to have attracted the attention that would have caused a great nation to record them. The significance that we retrospectively recognize in Israel derives from the religious heritage that it has given us, and not from its geopolitical standing in the Ancient Near East. From a worldly point of view, Israel would surely have been seen to have an inflated estimate of its importance. One way in which this grandiosity was conveyed in its Scripture was in the exaggeratedly large numbers with which its history is strewn, whether in relation to the numbers involved in the Exodus (Numbers 1) or the incredible life-spans attributed to people of the patriarchal period.

Jewish thinking divides its scriptures into three sections: the Law, the Prophets and the Writings. The Law (*Torah*) is contained in the Pentateuch, the first five books of the Hebrew Bible, called 'the Books of Moses'. There are several law codes in the Pentateuch, of which the oldest is thought to be the Book of the Covenant (Exodus 20—23), associated with the covenant made at Sinai between Israel and the Lord and containing the Ten Commandments. The code contains some primitively harsh injunctions, such as prescribing death for striking or cursing parents (21.15 and 17), but there are already also significant injunctions to mercy and compassionate care. Hebrew slaves are not to be bound to their masters for more than six years (21.2) and if physically abused they are to be released (21.26–27). The poor are to be treated with respect: 'If you take your neighbour's cloak in pawn, you shall return it before the sun goes down; for it may be your neighbour's only clothing to use as cover' (22.26). Although many commands relate only to the Hebrew community's internal care for its own members, there is also the injunction 'You shall not oppress the resident alien; you know the heart of an alien, for you were aliens in the land of Egypt' (23.9). Even enemies are to be treated properly. 'When you come upon your enemy's ox or donkey going astray, you shall bring it back' (23.4). The famous commandment to 'love your neighbour as yourself' (Leviticus 19.18) comes in a later stratum of the Law, which is called the Holiness Code, but the beginnings of this attitude can be found in the earlier text.

The section of the Hebrew Bible called the Prophets contains not only what we today would readily recognize as prophetic writings, such as Isaiah and Jeremiah, but also the 'Former Prophets', the books of our Bible from Joshua to 2 Kings. Although these books include stories of prophetic activities, most notably those of Elijah and Elisha, their general character strikes the contemporary reader as being that of a historical narrative. I suppose one might understand the inclusion of this extensive material under the rubric of prophecy as indicating that Israel saw the will of the Lord as being revealed as much through historical events as through explicit proclamations of judgement and hope.

The books of the 'Writing Prophets' that follow those of the Former Prophets are rich and complex. The ancient world did not have our modern concern for the identity and integrity of the work of an individual author. In consequence, a book with a single name attached to it may quite often contain material originating not only from its apparent initial author, but also from later writers working in the same tradition. The book of Isaiah illustrates this in a striking fashion. Scholars discern in it three distinct major blocks of material, originating at different times and in different circumstances. Chapters 1—39 are 'First Isaiah', principally associated with a prophet active in Jerusalem in the eighth century before Christ. Chapters 40—55 contain the message of 'Second Isaiah', a prophet of the period of the Exile who conveys a powerful assurance of God's continuing activity to bring about restoration and a new order. Chapters 56—66, 'Third Isaiah', centre on the hopes and fears of the post-Exilic period. Even simple study of an English translation will make these distinctions apparent to a careful reader.

The Former Prophets, who preceded the Writing Prophets, seem mostly to have operated in the context of the court and to be concerned with issuing warnings about political and religious policy addressed to the king. The later prophets address their message more widely to the whole nation, and they warn of judgements that will bring disaster on all. The Writing Prophets condemn repeated acts of national apostasy, the forsaking of the Lord to follow the false gods of Canaanite religion. They fearlessly denounce exploitation of the poor and the vulnerable. These prophets speak as messengers of God and characteristically they proclaim, 'Thus says the Lord ...'. The three major prophets in this section of the Hebrew Bible are Isaiah, Jeremiah and Ezekiel. Each gives an account of his original calling to the vocation of prophet.

Isaiah's call (Isaiah 6) comes in the famous vision he experiences in the Temple when he sees 'the Lord sitting on a throne, high and lofty' (v. 1). The prophet is overcome by a sense of his unworthiness to be found in this holy presence but, after a symbolic act of purgation by an angelic messenger, he is able to react to the divine question, 'Whom shall I send, and who will go for us?' by responding, 'Here am I; send me.' Immediately he is commissioned to go to the indifferent people of Israel who 'keep listening, but do not comprehend; keep looking but do not understand' (vv. 8–9).

When Jeremiah receives his call, he is reluctant to accept it. 'Ah, Lord God! Truly I do not know how to speak, for I am only a boy,' but the Lord says, 'You shall go to all to whom I send you, and you shall speak whatever I command you' (Jeremiah 1.6–7). Jeremiah is the prophet who suffers most because of the painfulness of his unsought vocation. 'Why is my pain unceasing, my wound incurable, refusing to be healed?' (Jeremiah 15.18, see also the bitter protest of Jeremiah 20.7–18). The book contains an extended narrative of how Jeremiah was persecuted for proclaiming the unwelcome message that Egypt would not deliver Jerusalem from the besieging armies of Babylon and that the king of Judah should hasten to make the best terms he could with Nebuchadnezzar while the chance was still there. Jeremiah is imprisoned for this defeatist message and is in danger of death (Jeremiah 34—39). The final irony is that after the defeat of Judah, some of the Jews still left in the land forcibly take Jeremiah to Egypt, the very country he has been warning them not to trust.

Ezekiel is in many ways the strangest of the major prophets and the book is full of powerful visions and weird symbolic acts. (Some have speculated that Ezekiel might have been a schizophrenic, a person in whom God made use of this particular circumstance for a particular purpose.) Ezekiel lived in Babylon among the exiles and his call came in an overwhelming vision he experienced beside the banks of the river Chebar (Ezekiel 1). A fiery chariot appeared with four strange living creatures and above them 'there was something like a throne in appearance like sapphire; and seated above the likeness of a throne was something that seemed like a human form . . . This was the appearance of the likeness of the glory of the LORD' (vv. 26 and 28). Ezekiel fell to the ground but he was commanded to stand up and he was despatched as God's messenger to the rebellious house of Israel.

The powerful imagery of Ezekiel has certainly influenced the book of Revelation in the New Testament, but the prophet who has most affected the thinking of Christianity has undoubtedly been Second Isaiah. We have already thought about the Servant Songs, which were understood by the Church to prefigure Christ, the crucified Messiah. In addition, there is a strong emphasis in Second Isaiah on God's freedom to act in new ways. 'Do not remember the former things, or consider the things of old. I am about to do a new thing; now it springs forth, do you not perceive it?' (Isaiah 43.18–19). The early Church was bound to find here an anticipation of the great new act that God had done in the life, death and resurrection of Jesus Christ.

People sometimes rightly remark that the prophets do not foretell but they forthtell. They have not been given a cinematic preview of the details of future history, but they have been afforded insight into the way that history is moving which enables them to warn of the consequences of disobedience to God and to offer promises of deliverance to those who will commit themselves to following the divine will. When Jeremiah told King Zedekiah to submit to Nebuchadnezzar, he had not been shown a trailer of the future event of the burning of the Temple, but he had been given the understanding to recognize that no salvation would be forthcoming from Egypt and that continued defiance of the Babylonians could only lead to some form of national disaster. The continuing vitality of the messages of the prophets for us today derives from the general understanding they convey of the purposes of God and the resulting divine activity that leads to both judgement and deliverance.

The third section of the Hebrew Bible, the Writings, almost inevitably has something of a miscellaneous character. It includes much material that was valued for its spiritual authority, but which did not seem to fit into the Law or the Prophets. We have already considered the wisdom writings, such as Proverbs and the book of Job. One of the books that the Hebrew Bible assigns to the Writings, the book of Daniel, is in fact included among the prophets in the Christian Bible. However, Daniel is obviously different in style and content from the other prophetic writings and only part of it was originally written in Hebrew, the rest being in Aramaic, a related language which, by the time of Jesus, had come to be the everyday speech in Palestine. In its present form Daniel was compiled in the second century before Christ, at a time when the successors of Alexander the Great ruled Judea and were seeking to impose Greek religious customs upon their Jewish subjects. This misguided attempt provoked a revolt led by the family of Judas Maccabaeus and the first part of Daniel (chs 2—6) consists of stories, such as the lions' den and the burning fiery furnace, clearly told to give encouragement to its Jewish readers to hold fast to God in the face of pagan persecution. The second part of Daniel (chs 7—12) has a quite different character. It gives accounts of visions, related in the style called apocalyptic. The word means 'unveiled' and the character of apocalyptic is to claim insight into the future of history, and beyond history, gained in the course of access to a special realm of heavenly truth. The most famous of these visions comes in chapter 7, when Daniel is shown a mysterious figure, the Son of Man, who appears before the Ancient of Days and is given 'dominion and glory and kingship, that all peoples, nations and languages should serve him' (vv. 13–14). In all the Gospels Jesus is portrayed as referring to the Son of Man, sometimes simply presented as a figure of divine authority and judgement but more often as seemingly a self-identification of Jesus himself. A great cloud of scholarly argument has gathered around what significance should be attributed to these facts, further complicated by the fact that the phrase 'son of man', strangely though it reads in English or Greek, is actually a perfectly natural Semitic way of simply saying 'human being'. This is not the place to go into this issue in any detail, though I have set out elsewhere what I make of it (see Further Reading).

The longest, and surely the most important, book in the Writings is the book of Psalms. Originating in the worship of the Jerusalem Temple, the Psalter has, for over a period of at least two and a half thousand years, been a profound liturgical resource for both Jews and Christians. The range of spiritual experience and expression to be found in its pages far exceeds that to be discovered within the covers of any hymn book. The psalmists write with great frankness and honesty, rejoicing in God's goodness but not afraid to protest in times of difficulty and suffering. Psalm 44 even tells God to wake up and pay attention to what is happening to Israel: 'Rouse yourself! Why do you sleep, O Lord? Awake, do not cast us off for ever' (v. 23). I believe that this spiritual realism about the seeming ambiguities of life has been an important factor in the enduring power and influence of the psalms.

There are hymns of praise for the goodness of creation (for example, Psalm 104), for deliverance (Psalm 114), for the joy of worshipping in Zion (Psalm 122). A frequent and powerful form of psalmody is the Lament. A lament psalm starts with protest at affliction, but it is able to end with renewed trust in the ultimate goodness of God. A perfect example of the Lament in miniature is Psalm 13, which begins 'How long, O Lord? Will you forget me for ever?' but ends 'I will sing to the Lord, because he has dealt bountifully with me'. I believe that the attainment of that final act of trust required the initial honesty of the acknowledgement of perplexity and the fear of abandonment. In some of the psalms one can surely recognize signs of how they might have been used in Temple worship. In Psalm 24, one can imagine a priest addressing a band of pilgrims with the question, 'Who shall ascend the hill of the Lord? And who shall stand in his holy place?', while the people preparing themselves to enter the holy precincts of the Temple respond, 'Those who have clean hands and pure hearts' (vv. 3–4). Later, when the priest cries, 'Who is the King of glory?', we can picture the people thundering out the reply, 'The Lord strong and mighty, the Lord mighty in battle' (v. 8). The longest, and perhaps the strangest, of the psalms is 119. In each of its 22 eight-verse stanzas, the lines all begin in Hebrew with the same letter of the alphabet, so that the psalm forms a huge acrostic from Aleph to Taw. Despite this highly artificial form, Psalm 119 is a magnificent meditation on the authority of the Torah, the Law of God.

The ambiguity of Scripture is illustrated by the 'cursing psalms', such as Psalm 58 and Psalm 109. Contemplating the wicked, the psalmist urges, 'O God, break the teeth in their mouths; tear out the fangs of the young lions' (58.6), followed by further verses in the same vein. Perhaps the most shocking of these psalms is 137, which after its tragic but beautiful opening, 'By the rivers of Babylon – there we sat down and there we wept when we remembered Zion', ends with the terrible verse addressed to the Babylonians, 'Happy shall they be that take your little ones and dash them against the rock'. Christians cannot make these words their own in worship. They can only serve as a reminder of the depth of evil that lurks in the human heart.

The Hebrew Bible was the scripture that permeated the thought of Jesus and the first Christians. It has the strange-nesses that come from its particular times and cultures, but it is also full of great riches. I believe that it is very important that the Old Testament retains its traditionally important place in the worship and thought of the Christian Church.

6

The Gospels

No literature in the ancient world has been subjected to such intense scholarly scrutiny as the four Gospels. For more than two hundred years, critical study has concentrated on seeking to analyse and evaluate what can reliably be learned from them about the historical Jesus of Nazareth. In the course of this intellectual activity, pretty well every conceivable answer has been given, ranging from 'practically nothing' to 'absolutely all that is necessary'. When I read the Gospels, I want to do so with my intellectual eyes open, but that certainly does not imply a strategy of relentless scepticism. People sometimes say that scientists doubt everything. To adopt such a stance would in fact be disastrous, for it would induce a kind of intellectual paralysis. The rational strategy is to commit oneself to what one considers to be well-motivated belief, while being aware that sometimes it may need revision in the light of further evidence and insight. This is the spirit in which I seek to approach the Gospels, but before doing so, I must make a remark about the authors' identities. The traditional assignments of Matthew, Mark, Luke and John only originate from statements made in the second century, where we are also told that Mark was closely associated with the apostle Peter and derived much of his material from him. There is much scholarly discussion about what to make of these claims, for the evidence they present is fragmentary and indirect. I think that the essential question is not the identity of the particular person who wrote a particular text, but the historical reliability of what was written. This is an issue to which we shall pay careful attention. For convenience, I shall use the traditional names to refer to the authors involved.

Even a casual reader will soon perceive that, while there is a good deal of similarity between Matthew, Mark and Luke (the 'Synoptic Gospels', so-called since they share a common point of view), John is distinctly different. In the Synoptics, Jesus is rooted in first-century Jewish life, giving much of his teaching in the form of homely parables and focussing his message on the coming of the Kingdom, the imminent rule of God. In John, Jesus speaks in timeless tones and much of what he has to say centres on himself. The series of 'I am' sayings – the bread of life (John 6.35), the light of the world (John 8.12), and so on – assert astonishing claims to unique and universal significance, and this attitude is reinforced by repeated depiction of himself as the Son sent by the Father and in intimate relationship with Him. Yet, the Jesus of John's Gospel is by no means simply a heavenly figure who only seems to appear in human form. The Prologue to the Gospel speaks of the Word who 'was with God and was God', but it also declares that 'the Word was made *flesh*' (John 1.1–14). The First Epistle of John, originating in the same school of thought as the Gospel and perhaps written by the same author, states that 'every spirit that confesses that Jesus Christ has come in the flesh is from God' and that those who deny that confession are not from God (1 John 4.2–3). When Jesus meets the woman of Samaria at the well, he is genuinely tired and thirsty and he has to ask her for a drink (John 4.3–14).

A strange feature of John's Gospel is the way in which it refers only obliquely to important events that are described explicitly in the Synoptics. For example, Jesus' baptism by John the Baptist, an event of central significance for Matthew, Mark and Luke, is simply alluded to (John 1.32). In the account of the Last Supper, the footwashing stands in the place of the institution of Holy Communion (John 13.3–11), though there is teaching of clear Eucharistic significance given in the context of the feeding of the five thousand (John 6.52–58). No account is given of Gethsemane and it is simply said that Jesus and his disciples entered a garden before the arrest (John 18.1). Readers of John will only fully understand what is happening if they have also read one of the Synoptics. Why there should be this Johannine reticence is not clear to me. Another example of John's inclination to take an oblique approach is provided by the references to an unidentified 'beloved disciple' (13.23; 21.7 and 20). It is often believed that they are somewhat coy references to the disciple who was either the author of the Gospel or the one whose testimony forms its basis (see 21.24).

There are some disagreements between John and the Synoptics about the timing of events. The latter place Jesus' act of cleansing the Temple in the last week of his life, while John locates it during a visit to Jerusalem at the start of the public ministry. This difference may be explained by the fact that John, plausibly enough, recounts three visits by Jesus to Jerusalem, while the Synoptics only record the final visit. There is also a famous disagreement about the dating of the crucifixion. All the Gospels agree that it took place on a Friday, but the Synoptics say that it was the Day of the Passover, while John says that it was the Day of Preparation, preceding the Passover itself. A theological motive may well be at work here, for the Day of Preparation was the day on which the Passover lambs were slaughtered in the Temple and for John it is the fitting day on which the Lamb of God should die for the sins of the world.

The similarities between the Synoptics stem from the fact that they share much material in common. A great deal of Mark's Gospel reappears in Matthew and Luke, sometimes with interesting small changes of detail. (This is one reason why most scholars believe Mark to be the earliest Gospel, from which Matthew and Luke subsequently copied.) We have already noted that Matthew and Luke have in common a substantial body of material relating to the sayings of Jesus, material not found in Mark and which many scholars believe comes from an earlier document Q. In addition, there is material that is distinctive either to Matthew or to Luke. For example, the parables of the Good Samaritan and the Prodigal Son appear only in Luke.

In understanding the Gospels, it is important to realize that they are not biographies written in a modern manner. Not only do they omit much that such biographies would contain (What did Jesus look like?), but also, in the ancient world, writings about an important person were selective and concentrated simply on what was of central significance for the character portrayed. Moreover, there was not the modern concern to be absolutely accurate about matters of subsidiary detail. This latter point is strikingly illustrated by the three accounts given in Acts of the conversion of Paul on the road to Damascus (Acts 9.1–9; 22.6–11; 26.12–18). Despite the fact that they come from the pen of the same author and are included in the same book, they give different answers to the questions: Did all see the heavenly light? Did all hear the heavenly voice? Did all fall to the ground?

Despite these minor differences, it is clear that all the accounts are telling the same essential story. The point to get across is the total transformation of Paul's life that followed his encounter with the risen Christ.

The essential point that the Gospels are seeking to get across is expressed in John, where it is said, 'these things are written so that you may come to believe that Jesus is the Messiah, the Son of God, and that through believing you may have life in his name' (20.31). This concentration on what is primary means that we should not look in the Gospels for complete consistency of subsidiary detail in what they have to say. All three Synoptics tell a story of the curing of blindness in an incident associated with the city of Jericho. In Matthew (20.29–34), it involves two men encountered on the way out of the city. In Mark (10.46–52), it is one man, met as Jesus and the disciples are leaving. In Luke (18.35–43), it is one man met on entry. Clearly, all three are telling essentially the same story, whose deeper significance is that meeting with Jesus brings people out of darkness into light. We may easily imagine these differences of detail arising in the period of oral transmission that preceded the assembly of the stories in consolidated written form.

I think that we have good reason to believe that the evangelists were seeking to tell a reliable story of what happened, expressed within the historical conventions of their time. One sign of this is that they record sayings of Jesus which must have been problematic for them, but which had to be included in a truthful account. In Mark (10.17–22), a man comes to Jesus and asks him, 'Good Teacher, what must I do to inherit eternal life?' Jesus responds by saying, 'Why do you call me good? No one is good but God alone.' Since the early

Church believed that Jesus was sinless, this saying must have seemed a hard one to understand, but it had to be reported because it was there in the tradition. Matthew 19.17 in fact tones it down to the innocuous 'Why do you ask me about what is good?', but Luke (18.19) decided that the difficult form had to be retained. All four Gospels tell the story of Peter's threefold denial of Jesus, a highly embarrassing incident in the life of one of the leaders of the early Church, which nevertheless had to be recorded because it was what had actually happened. Both Matthew 27.46 and Mark 15.34 are honest enough to report the cry of dereliction from the cross, 'My God, my God, why have you forsaken me?' Mark feels that this is of such solemn significance that he must record the actual Aramaic words that Jesus would have spoken, 'Eloi, Eloi, lema sabachthani?', but Matthew reduces the shock a little by turning the words into Hebrew, suggesting a quotation of Psalm 22.1. One further example of the evangelists' honesty of reporting must suffice. Matthew 10.23 tells of Jesus sending out the disciples with the words, 'I tell you, you will not have gone through all the towns of Israel before the Son of Man comes.' Matthew was probably writing about fifty years after the despatch of the disciples, when it must have been clear that, at least in a straightforward historical sense of the words, they had not been fulfilled. Nevertheless, the saying had to be included in his Gospel.

Another indication of the carefulness of the Gospel writers to convey the tradition they had received, seems to me to be found in a handful of incidents whose significance now escapes us, but which presumably the evangelists felt had for some reason to be preserved. Examples would be the odd story of the young man who fled naked from Gethsemane (Mark 14.51–52) and the strange manner in which Nathanael is so impressed when Jesus says that he saw him under a fig tree (John 1.48).

If these considerations persuade us, as I believe they should, to take the truthful intent of the evangelists with due seriousness, they will lead us to go on to enquire what we can reliably learn about Jesus from the Gospels. We shall be concerned with finding out both what he said and what he did. Let us begin with the former. We shall be looking for signs of a distinctive personality revealed in the sayings material.

Surely the first thing that strikes one is Jesus' use of parables. While many people use stories to help communicate what they want to say, the pithy and pointed character of the parables seems to be something special. It is very difficult to devise concise stories that have the haunting impact on the reader of such parables as the Prodigal Son (Luke 15.11–32) or the Sheep and Goats (Matthew 25.31–46). I do not think that these stories simply come from a variety of anonymous authors who made them up in the scattered communities of the early Church. Rather, they are the creations of a single person of genius. Jesus clearly had a remarkable gift in this respect.

Next, one might look for certain turns of phrase that are repeated and which seem to be characteristic of him. One of these is the familiar word 'Amen', the Hebrew for 'May it be so'. First-century Jews would use the word as we do, as an affirmation of consent and commitment at the end of a prayer. In all four Gospels, Jesus uses it quite differently, placing it at the beginning of a sentence as the assertion that what he says will indeed be the case (for example, in the Sermon on the Mount: Matthew 5.18 and 26). This usage is exclusive to Jesus in the Gospels, but unfortunately it is somewhat disguised in many English translations, where it is often rendered 'Verily' or 'Truly', thereby reducing something of its unique force. This usage surely signifies that Jesus believed that he was speaking with an altogether exceptional authority. Another characteristic phrase, to which we have referred already, is 'the Son of Man'. Again, all four Gospels attribute its use solely to Jesus (the exception of John 12.34 is simply the crowd echoing Jesus' words back to him). Elsewhere in the New Testament it is only used by Stephen in relation to the heavenly vision he sees at the time of his martyrdom (Acts 7.56), and twice, significantly without the definite article in the Greek, in Revelation (1.13; 14.14). I have already noted the scholarly disagreements about how to interpret these facts, but it seems to me that this association with Jesus, and the absence of any evidence for its currency otherwise in the early Church, surely indicate that a special significance attaches to the phrase in the thinking of Jesus himself, and I believe that it refers back to Daniel 7. This would imply a claim to an exceptional role in the fulfilment of the purposes of God. These considerations indicate the presence in the Synoptics of a self-understanding in Jesus not wholly unlike that expressed in the much more explicit claims made in the 'I am' sayings in John. I do not think that the latter, in the form in which John gives them, are likely to have been uttered by Jesus in his earthly lifetime, but I believe that they have arisen from deep reflection, in the light of the Resurrection, on the inner meaning of that life. It would be in accord with the conventions of historical writing in the ancient world to convey the true significance of the person being written about in just such a way.

Despite these signs of special status and authority, the Gospels make it clear that throughout his life Jesus needed to pray to his heavenly Father, seeking to know God's will and to be given divine strength for the fulfilment of his vocation. This necessity finds its deepest and most moving expression in the story of Gethsemane (Matthew 26.36–46; Mark 14.32–42; Luke 22.40–46 – we have noted that John, in his oblique way, only mentions that Jesus and the disciples entered a garden). This is surely one of the most profound incidents in the gospel narrative, as Jesus experiences a very human reluctance at the prospect of imminent suffering and death, but finds the strength to accept his Father's will. In Mark's account Jesus uses the Aramaic word 'Abba' in his address to the Father. (The word recurs elsewhere in the New Testament in Romans 8.15 and Galatians 4.6.) It is a word that carries a tone of family intimacy. Although it appears explicitly only once in the Gospels, we may suppose that it often lay behind Jesus' frequent references to God as Father. Many think that *abba* would have been the opening word of the Lord's prayer in the original Aramaic.

One final example of the striking character of the discourse of Jesus can be found in the manner in which he often dealt with hostile questioners. In such encounters as the issue of paying tax to Caesar, the dispute with the Sadducees about a destiny beyond death, and the character of the Messiah (Mark 12.13–27, 35–37), he displays an incisive ability to cut through superficial argument to get to the heart of the matter, in a manner that confronts the questioner with what is really at stake. Here again I think we see the sign of a remarkable individual mind at work.

I have already indicated that I do not suppose, however, that every word attributed in the Gospels to Jesus was actually spoken by him in his earthly life. The custom of the ancient world was such that it would not have been considered fraudulent to attribute to a historical character words he might have said in a particular circumstance, even if it was not part of that character's actual experience, provided it was thought that the statement was compatible with what the character would have been expected to say had he been in that situation. A likely example of this in the Gospels is found in Matthew 18.15–17. Jesus is portrayed as giving instructions about how to deal with disagreement in the Church. (Although common elsewhere in the New Testament, this and 16.18 are the only places where the Greek word *ekklesia* is found in the Gospels.) I think it is likely that this saying corresponds to what Matthew thought Jesus would have said had he been faced with that particular problem. However, it is also the case that the Gospel writers appear to have been very sparing in their use of this freedom. Acts and Paul make it clear that an issue that greatly exercised the early Church was whether male gentile converts had to be circumcised on their conversion to the Christian Way. It would have been easy to invent a word of Jesus settling the matter, but no such word is to be found in the Gospels.

A more contentious example concerns the nature of the 'passion predictions'. The Synoptics tell us that Jesus on his way to Jerusalem three times warned his disciples that he was to be rejected and killed, and that he told them that after three days he would rise again (Mark 8.31; 9.31; 10.33–34; and parallels). Many scholars believe that these are predictions after the event, inserted by the evangelists with the benefit of hindsight. I think that the matter is more complex than that. I do not doubt that the precise wording of these predictions has been influenced by later events, particularly in the case of the reference to the Resurrection, but I do not believe that

Jesus lacked the insight to recognize that his presence in Jerusalem would bring about a violent confrontation with the authorities, or that he did not have the faith to trust himself to God for his eventual vindication. It is entirely reasonable to suppose that Jesus sought to share these thoughts with his disciples, even if they found them hard to understand and accept at that time.

A somewhat related matter is the extent to which the evangelists were influenced in what they wrote by a desire to show that Jesus fulfilled Old Testament prophecy. The Gospel with the strongest emphasis on this theme is Matthew. However, it is a very strange assortment of texts to which he appeals, ranging from the most general kind of allusion (for example, Matthew 8.17, quoting Isaiah with reference to acts of healing) to a text illegitimately manipulated in its meaning (Matthew 2.15, where a verse from Hosea, clearly referring to the Exodus, is alleged to relate to the flight of the holy family into Egypt). It is understandable that the early Church sought to connect its knowledge of Christ with what it read in the Hebrew scriptures, but my impression is that it is the actual life of Jesus that shapes the evangelists' use of the Hebrew Bible, rather than the story being forced to conform to this oddly eclectic selection of Old Testament texts. This judgement receives some confirmation from the fact that New Testament writers are quite free in the way in which they use the Hebrew Bible. For example, Matthew 3.3, Mark 1.3 and Luke 3.4 all cite Isaiah 40.3 in relation to John the Baptist, but they repunctuate the Hebrew, so that instead of reading 'a voice cries out, "In the wilderness prepare the way of the Lord"', the text is made to fit the facts by being turned into 'the voice of one crying out in the wilderness: "Prepare the way of the Lord"'.

We need also to recognize that there are words of Jesus that are 'hard sayings', with which we have to struggle in various ways. I shall take most of my examples from Mark, though there are usually parallel passages in Matthew and Luke.

First there are the sayings that uncompromisingly challenge the reader with the cost of discipleship, making it clear that to follow Christ will be a demanding vocation. A familiar example is the saying Jesus addresses to his followers, 'let them deny themselves and take up their cross and follow me' (Mark 8.34). These words make uncomfortable reading, but they simply reflect the reality that discipleship will demand discipline and sacrifice.

Other hard sayings arise in the context of disputes with the scribes and Pharisees, who are frequently condemned and called 'hypocrites' (e.g. Mark 7.6–13). What may trouble us here is the uncompromisingly severe way in which Jesus seems to express himself, in notable contrast with his ready acceptance of publicans and sinners. 'Gentle Jesus' is certainly not an appropriate description. The severity of the condemnation is particularly strong in Matthew, for example in the long series of woes proclaimed in 23.13–36 and in the characterization of his opponents as 'a brood of vipers' (12.34). We need to bear in mind here that in Hebrew tradition there was a strong tendency to impart emphasis by expressing matters in extreme terms of black and white. Thus in Malachi 1.2–3, the divine choice among the two sons of Isaac is expressed by God saying, 'I have loved Jacob but I have hated Esau.' In John (8.12–59; 10.19–37) there is also much bitter and intense controversy, but the opponents here are simply called 'the Jews'.

There are sayings of Jesus about judgement in which he speaks in a manner that the modern reader may find disturbing. For example, in Mark 9.42–48, there are warnings of the danger of being 'thrown into hell [literally, in the Greek, Gehenna, the ever-burning rubbish dump outside Jerusalem], where their worm never dies and the fire is never quenched'. The fact that this warning is coupled with injunctions such as cutting off a hand that offends, shows that once again the Semitic tendency to extreme expression is surely at work. Nevertheless, there is an undeniable sternness in Jesus' pronouncements of moral judgement. These are not matters to be taken lightly. In Matthew 10.28, he says, 'Do not fear those who kill the body but cannot kill the soul; rather fear him who can destroy both soul and body in hell [Gehenna].'

Finally there is the long apocalyptic passage in Mark 12, with parallels in Matthew 24 and Luke 21, which seems to speak of the eventual destruction of the Temple (which actually happened in AD 70 at the hands of the Romans) and of an end-time of catastrophic woes and suffering to be followed by the deliverance of the elect. The language and style are strange indeed to modern ears. A hundred years ago, New Testament scholars, such as Albert Schweitzer, tended so to emphasize this element in the Gospels that they pictured Jesus principally as an eschatological prophet whose predictions failed to receive immediate fulfilment. Today, scholars argue about how much of this apocalyptic material goes back to Jesus himself and how much originated in the activity of prophets in the early Church. Whatever the rights of this may be, I think that it is clear that there was warning and urgency in Jesus' proclamation of the coming of the Kingdom of God, which served to underline the intense seriousness of the choices he was demanding that his hearers should make.

Perhaps the most certain fact about the deeds of Jesus is that he was an outstanding healer. There are many healing stories in the Gospels and they could not be excised without destroying the whole fabric of the narrative. A repeated theme is controversy about the propriety of healing on the Sabbath. This was clearly a point of sharp contention between Jesus and the Jewish authorities and this could not have been the case unless there actually were such healings. Quite often these healings are depicted in terms of exorcism, the casting out of evil spirits (Mark 1.21–28, 32–34 and so on). Of course this is not how we would understand them today. It is important to remember that Jesus was truly a first-century Jew and so he and his contemporaries naturally interpreted his deeds in terms of the idiom of their day.

Jesus is also credited with other remarkable deeds. The general theological issue of miracle is not one that I wish to pursue in any detail here (see Further Reading). John's Gospel insists that miraculous acts are to be understood as 'signs', that is, they are windows through which one can look more deeply into the reality of what God was doing in Christ. They are not to be treated as if they were simply a series of stories of wonder-working. To be theologically credible, miracles must be revelatory events, not capricious conjuring tricks. Some of the gospel miracles can be understood as manifestations of human powers possessed by Jesus to a pre-eminent degree, such as acts of psychosomatic healing. Others might be natural events with a revelatory significance due to the providential timing of their occurrence (for instance, the stilling of the storm, Mark 4.37–41). The only miracle that is unambiguously recorded in all four Gospels is the feeding of the multitude (Mark 6.33–44; 8.1–10; and parallels). It is a story with obvious theological overtones, in relation to the

Jewish concept of the Messianic Banquet and in relation to the Christian sacrament of Holy Communion. It seems to me that it is almost impossible to visualize what actually happened. The suggestion that the crowd were persuaded to share the picnics that they had been concealing for private enjoyment, seems pathetically lame. The key Christian miracle is, of course, the Resurrection. It will be the concern of the chapter that follows.

Another fact about Jesus that it seems impossible to doubt is his willingness to accept, and even eat with, disreputable sinners, including tax collectors and prostitutes (see, for example, Mark 2.13–17). This behaviour scandalized his Jewish contemporaries, who strongly disapproved of his acting in this way without first insisting on a public act of repentance.

I have left till last what are among the best-known and best-loved narratives in the Gospels: the stories of the birth of Jesus. We find them only in Matthew 1.18—2.12 and Luke 2.1–20. John, after his timeless Prologue, and Mark, without any preliminaries, both start with the encounters between John the Baptist and Jesus at the beginning of the public ministry. We are so used to conflating the two gospel accounts that it is only when we read them carefully and separately that we become aware of how different they are. Luke seems to tell the story very much from the point of view of Mary, and the visitors to the newborn Jesus are the humble shepherds. Matthew seems to see things much more from Joseph's perspective, and his visitors are the magi. Much of our pictorial imaging of the birth arises from fusing these two narratives in a manner heavily influenced by carols and by the many paintings made by artists. There is no reason to believe that the magi were kings; rather they were

Eastern astrological sages. We are not even told that there were three of them. This traditional belief arises from the threefold gifts of gold, frankincense and myrrh. Luke gives us a very specific dating of the birth in relation to a Roman census, but there are severe scholarly difficulties in reconciling this with what is known of ancient history and with Matthew's (plausible) statement that it took place during the reign of King Herod the Great. A principal concern in both narratives is to explain why, if Mary's home was at Nazareth, Jesus was born in Bethlehem, as Messianic prophecy required. I do not doubt that there is historical truth preserved in the birth stories, but establishing its exact content is not an easy task.

Luke, very explicitly in his story of the Annunciation (1.34–35), and Matthew, more obliquely (1.18), both assert the virginal conception of Jesus. Christian tradition has attached great significance to this, often rather inaccurately calling it the 'virgin birth'. Yet in the New Testament it seems nowhere near as widely significant as the Resurrection. Paul is content simply to lay stress on Jesus' solidarity with humanity: 'God sent his Son, born of woman, born under the law' (Galatians 4.4). The theological importance of the virginal conception lies in its lending emphasis to the presence of a total divine initiative in the coming of Jesus, even if this truth is much more frequently expressed by New Testament writers simply in the language of his having been sent. Jesus was not opportunistically co-opted for God's purpose when he was found to be suitable, but he was part of that purpose from the start. The virginal conception is a powerful myth, and I believe that in the religion of the Incarnation the power of story fuses with the power of a true story, so that the great Christian myths are *enacted* myths.

On this basis, I find myself able to believe in the virgin birth, even if the motivating evidence is less extensive than that for belief in the Resurrection.

I believe that if we look at the Gospels carefully, as I have been trying to do, we shall see that they give us an authentic portrait of the man who stands behind their narrative, someone whom the distinguished New Testament scholar, Charlie Moule, characterized as 'a personality striking, original, baffling yet illuminating'. I agree with his assessment, for I find in Jesus' words and deeds a challenge and a hope that I absolutely must make central to my own search for a truthful understanding of the nature of reality.

It is not difficult to believe that Jesus drew large crowds and excited high hopes. Yet, that first Good Friday, it must have seemed that all that promise had ended in failure, with the spectacle of a deserted leader suffering the painful and shameful death of crucifixion and crying out from the darkness of his place of execution, 'My God, my God, why have you forsaken me?' If that really was the end for Jesus, I honestly believe that we would never have heard of him. He would have seemed to have been yet another first-century Messianic pretender who, in the end, proved to be the victim of illusory ambitions. But we have all heard about Jesus. Something happened to continue his story. What that something was is a question that we shall have to investigate in the chapter that follows.

7

Cross and Resurrection

In the early chapters of the Gospels, the verbs associated with Jesus are in the active voice, relating to his authoritative words and powerful deeds in the course of his public ministry. However, when the narrative reaches the final week in Jerusalem, the voice changes and the verbs become passive. Things happen to Jesus, as he is subjected to an unjust trial and handed over to suffering and death. The Gospels all attach the most profound significance to this last week. In Mark, it occupies six of the 16 chapters.

Crucifixion was devised by the Romans to be a lingering and torturing death, imposed on rebels, slaves and felons. To the criminal hanging on the cross, every breath was excruciating as he had to press on the nails to raise his chest in order to breathe. The perpetual pain, together with the loss of blood, the heat, the flies and the public exposure, made crucifixion a particularly horrible form of death. Eventually, after hours of struggle, the victim gave up trying to breathe and died of asphyxiation. If necessary, the soldiers would finally break the legs of the criminals to prevent them being able to struggle further (cf. John 19.32). In addition to this suffering, a first-century Jew would have seen crucifixion as a sign of divine rejection, for it says in Deuteronomy 21.23, 'anyone hung on a tree is under God's curse'. Throughout the Roman world crucifixion was regarded with such horror that 'cross' (Greek *stauros*) was a word of sinister meaning to a degree that it is hard for us to recapture, since for us it has come to mean simply a conventional religious symbol. There is no depiction of the crucified Christ in Christian art until the centuries in which crucifixion was no longer a contemporary reality. The earliest Christians preferred to represent Jesus as the Good Shepherd.

Crucifixion is the death that Jesus died, after crying out, 'My God, my God, why have you forsaken me?' I have already acknowledged that a contemporary that first Good Friday, looking at the figure nailed to the tree, would simply have felt that he saw a Messianic pretender whose grandiose claims had proved to be empty. Yet the centurion in charge of the execution apparently felt that he saw something quite different from the routine death of a malefactor, with which he must have been very familiar. Mark 15.39 tells us that he exclaimed, 'Truly this man was God's Son!'; Luke 23.47 says that he praised God and said, 'Certainly this man was innocent.'

If Jesus was indeed raised from the dead to a life of unending glory, then the centurion was right, the transformation of the frightened disciples into fearless proclaimers of the Lordship of Jesus is explained, and we can understand why the story of Jesus has continued so powerfully down to the present day. We need to investigate whether there is evidence that might rightly motivate us to believe that this was indeed the case. The first point to emphasize is the magnitude of the claim being made. There are stories in the Gospels of persons who were apparently dead being restored to life (Jairus' daughter, Mark 5.35–43 and parallels; the son of the widow of Nain, Luke 7.11–17; Lazarus, John 11.38–44).

However, these are resuscitations, that is to say, those so restored will undoubtedly in due course die again. They have only experienced a temporary reprieve from mortality, somewhat like people in our own day who have had near-death experiences. Jesus' resurrection is quite different. He is given a permanent victory over death. In the opening vision of the book of Revelation, the risen Christ is portrayed as the one who proclaims, 'I was dead, and see, I am alive for ever and ever and I have the keys of Death and Hades' (1.18). Many Jews in the first century believed that there would be a general resurrection of the dead to everlasting life at the end of history, but no one expected this to occur to a single individual within history. The idea of a resurrected Messiah in this absolute sense would have been as strange to a first-century Jew as the idea of a crucified Messiah, and as strange as resurrection seems to many people today.

The earliest statement of the Resurrection that we have occurs in the Pauline writings, which predate the Gospels. Writing to the Corinthians about the year 55, Paul reminds them that

> Christ died for our sins in accordance with the scriptures, that he was buried, and that he was raised on the third day in accordance with the scriptures, and that he appeared to Cephas, then to the twelve. Then he appeared to more than five hundred brothers and sisters at one time, most of whom are still alive, though some have died. Then he appeared to James, then to all the apostles. Last of all, as to someone untimely born, he appeared also to me.   (1 Corinthians 15.3–8)

When Paul refers to 'what I had in turn received', it is natural to suppose that he is referring to teaching he received after his dramatic conversion on the road to Damascus. This

73

would take the quoted testimony back to within a very few years of the events themselves, and this antiquity receives some confirmation in the use of the Aramaic 'Cephas' for Peter and the reference to the apostles as 'the twelve', usages that soon died out in the early Christian community. Although the concise list of witnesses, most still living, makes it clear that Paul's intent is to give evidential support to his belief in Jesus as his living Lord, the condensed character of the passage gives us little clue to what these appearance experiences might have been like. To gain further insight we have to turn to the Gospels.

We immediately encounter a confusing scene. Mark does not include an actual appearance story, despite his Gospel (14.28, 16.7) twice giving a promise that the risen Christ will meet with the disciples in Galilee. (The concluding verses (16.9–20) given in many English versions are known to be second-century additions and do not offer any independent evidence.) Scholars debate whether the original Gospel was intended to end as abruptly as 16.8, or whether there were further verses, now lost. In Matthew there is a brief story of an appearance to the women returning from the tomb, but the main appearance takes place in Galilee (28.9–10, 16–20). In Luke everything seems to happen in Jerusalem that first Easter Day (24.13–50), though the same author in Acts 1.3 speaks of appearances taking place over a period of 40 days. In John there are appearances in Jerusalem (20.11–29) and in Galilee (21.1–23). This variety contrasts with the essential similarities between the Gospels in their accounts of the last week of Jesus' life, even if there are differences among them about the exact nature of the trial that he underwent.

At first sight it might seem that we are simply confronted with a bunch of variously made-up tales, constructed by different Christian communities as ways of expressing their conviction that in some way Jesus continued to be their living Lord. However, there is an unexpected and persistent feature of the stories, expressed in different ways, that persuades me that their historicity needs to be taken seriously. This feature is that initially it was difficult to recognize the risen Christ for who he was. Mary Magdalene took him to be the gardener (John 20.15). The couple on the way to Emmaus did not know who their companion was until at the very end when he broke bread with them before disappearing from their sight (Luke 24.30–31). On the lake in Galilee, only the beloved disciple had the insight to recognize the figure standing on the shore (John 21.7). With astonishing frankness, Matthew tells us that when Jesus appeared on that Galilean hillside, there were still some who doubted (28.17). Most of the stories climax in a moment of recognition when it dawns on the participants who they are with. This seems to me to be a very unlikely feature to be found in a collection of independently made-up tales. I believe that it is an actual historical reminiscence of what those encounters were like, and so I conclude that the appearance stories have real evidential value and need to be taken with great seriousness.

A second line of evidence is of course presented in the Gospels, which all tell the story of the discovery of the empty tomb (Matthew 28.1–8; Mark 16.1–8; Luke 24.1–10; John 20.1–10). There is a good deal of agreement between these gospel accounts, even if there are differences about such details as the names of the women and the exact time of morning they made their discovery. It is striking that the initial reaction of the women is not joy but fear. They were not expecting resurrection and hence the need, expressed in somewhat different ways in each of the Gospels, for some form of angelic message to make the significance clear. However, there are a number of problems that need to be discussed before the value of the evidence of the empty tomb stories can properly be assessed.

The first is whether there was, in fact, an identifiable tomb at all. It was common Roman practice to bury executed criminals (which is what Jesus would have seemed to the authorities to be) in an anonymous common grave, or even to leave their bodies to be eaten by wild animals. Yet we know from archaeological evidence that this was not an invariable custom. A reason for accepting that in the case of Jesus there was such a tomb is that in all four Gospels Joseph of Arimathea is credited with providing it. He is otherwise an unknown figure of no subsequent significance in the early Christian movement and the best reason for his association with this courageous and honourable act is surely to believe that he actually did it.

A second problem is that Paul makes no reference to the empty tomb in his epistles. Yet these are occasional writings, composed to deal with specific situations, and there must have been many things that Paul knew which he did not need to tell his readers for the particular purpose of the letter. Moreover, many think that it is significant that in that very condensed account in 1 Corinthians 15, Paul took the trouble to say that Jesus was buried. This may well indicate that Paul knew that there was a tomb and that a special significance attached to it. It is certainly the case that a first-century Jew like Paul, with a strongly embodied concept of the human person, would not have believed that Jesus was truly alive, as he undoubtedly did believe, if his body in fact lay mouldering in a tomb.

There is a further consideration that strengthens belief in the empty tomb. In the early history of conflict between the Church and the Jewish community about the significance of Jesus, it is common ground that there was a tomb and that it was empty, and the argument about why this was so can be traced back into the first century itself (cf. Matthew 28.13–15). The disagreement was about whether the tomb was empty because the disciples had stolen the body in an act of deceit, or because Jesus had truly risen from the dead. It seems to me that the idea of apostolic deceit is simply incredible in view of their later steadfast Christian confession, even to the point of martyrdom. Equally unconvincing is the suggestion that the women just made a mistake and went to the wrong tomb. The authorities would then soon have acted to quash the troublesome Christian movement by exhibiting the real tomb with its corpse inside, if that had been the case.

But the most powerful argument for the authenticity of the empty tomb is that it is the women who are the witnesses. In the ancient world women were not regarded as being reliable witnesses in a court of law and anyone simply making up a tale would make sure it was men who played the key role in it. The women are there, I believe, because they were indeed the ones who made this startling discovery.

There is, therefore, evidential motivation for believing that Jesus was indeed raised from the dead. How one weighs that evidence will, however, also depend on how such a counter-intuitive belief (in fact as unexpected in the first century as it is in ours) might be accommodated within one's world view of the nature of reality. Those who are committed to an unrevisable belief in the absolute uniformity of nature will be driven to invoke the category of legend as the only way to interpret the gospel stories. However, to take this stance is to approach the scripture with a mind already closed to what it has to say. The whole of the New Testament is predicated upon the understanding that there is something unique about Jesus. If he was just yet another wandering rabbi or failed prophet, no doubt he remained dead. But if God was indeed present in Christ in a unique way, then his story may rationally be believed to contain unique elements. For the Christian believer, the Resurrection makes sense because it represents a triple vindication. It is the vindication of Jesus, for his life had a character that meant that it should not have ended in rejection and failure. It is a vindication of God, who was not found after all to have abandoned the one who had wholly committed himself to doing his Father's will. It is a vindication of a deep-seated human intuition that in the end the last word does not lie with death and futility, but we live in a world that is a meaningful cosmos and not ultimately a meaningless chaos. Christians see the resurrection of Christ as the sign and guarantee within history of a destiny that awaits the rest of humanity beyond history ('for as all die in Adam, so all will be made alive in Christ', 1 Corinthians 15.22).

The earliest Christians were Jews, yet the first day of the week came to be the special Christian day, in contrast to the orthodox Jewish Sabbath. This was because it was believed to be the day on which the Lord had risen from the tomb. I believe that this is a belief that we can still embrace today as one of the foundations of the Christian faith.

Associated with the Resurrection is the story of the Ascension. Only Luke gives an explicit account, both in the Gospel (24.51), where it seems to happen on Easter Day, and a more extended account in Acts (1.6–11), where it is said to happen

40 days after the Resurrection. This difference in dating indicates clearly that what is involved is not the story of a simple historical event, but something with heavy symbolic significance. The cloud that is said to have received Jesus out of the sight of the disciples is not a meteorological phenomenon but, as often in Scripture (Exodus 19.16; Daniel 7.13; Mark 9.7), a symbol of the divine presence. The Ascension is not Jesus starting out on some curious space-journey, but signifies his return to the Father and his taking up exalted authority (to use another symbolic image) as he is seated at the right hand of the throne of God (Hebrews 8.1). Although the other Gospels do not refer to the Ascension, the statement of the risen Christ at the end of Matthew (28.18) that he has been given 'all authority in heaven and on earth' is another expression of the same theological truth.

8

The Pauline writings

The earliest New Testament writings are the epistles of the apostle Paul. The first letter to the Thessalonians is usually considered to be the first of these writings and to have been written about the year 50. (The crucifixion was in either 30 or 33.) Already Jesus is being described in exalted terms as 'God's Son from heaven, whom he raised from the dead' (1.10). In Hebrew thinking, the phrase 'son of God' did not necessarily carry a divine connotation, for it could be used of the king of Israel (see Psalm 2.7), but the idea that Jesus had been sent from heaven surely justifies spelling 'Son' with a capital letter in this verse. The most common title assigned to Jesus in the Pauline writings is 'Lord', occurring well over two hundred times. Although the Greek *kyrios* could amount to no more than a courtesy in common conversation, much like the English use of 'sir', its presence in such theological contexts as Paul's letters surely carries with it an inescapable reference to the Jewish custom of saying 'Lord' in place of the unutterable name of God. It is, therefore, highly significant that the earliest distinctively Christian confession appears to have been 'Jesus is Lord' (Romans 10.9; 1 Corinthians 12.3; Philippians 2.11). It is also striking that Paul begins almost all his letters with the greeting, 'Grace to you and peace from God our Father and the Lord Jesus Christ' (Romans 1.7;

1 Corinthians 1.3, etc.). Despite his being a monotheistic Jew, Paul is bracketing together God and Jesus in an extraordinary way. One could not imagine a Jew conjoining God and Moses in such a fashion.

There are people who believe that this Lordship language is an example of the way in which Paul, influenced by his contacts with the Greek world, distorted Christianity from its origin in the words of an unpretentious wandering rabbi and turned it into something like a mystery religion of divine power. However, there are good scholarly reasons for rejecting this tendentious thesis. For example, in 1 Corinthians 16.22, Paul quotes verbatim the Aramaic phrase *Maran atha* (Our Lord come), clearly treating it as a saying that would be familiar to his readers. Surely, this indicates that even in the earliest, Aramaic-speaking, stratum of the Christian community, the Lordship of Jesus was acknowledged. Lordship language appears to be ineradicable from the New Testament witness. Prayers to Jesus seem to have been a feature of early Christianity. Writing to the Corinthians, Paul speaks of 'all those who in every place call on the name of our Lord Jesus Christ, both their Lord and ours' (1 Corinthians 1.2). When he is seeking the removal of some troublesome condition that he calls a 'thorn in the flesh', it is to the Lordship and power of Christ that Paul appeals (2 Corinthians 12.7–10).

In a celebrated passage that is the earliest New Testament account of the institution by Jesus of Holy Communion, Paul tells the Corinthians that he 'received from the Lord what I also handed on to you, that the Lord Jesus on the night when he was betrayed took a loaf of bread . . .', going on to quote those mysterious words, 'This is my body that is for you . . . This cup is the new covenant in my blood', and to convey the command to 'do this . . . in remembrance of me' (1 Corinthians 11.23–26). In their way, these words are as remarkable as the 'I am' sayings in John.

It seems to me that Paul, in common with the other New Testament writers, is struggling to find words to express his experience of the risen Christ and in the course of that he is being driven, despite his Jewish monotheism, to use both human and divine-sounding language about Jesus. A theologian has described this stance as amounting to 'binitarian monotheism'. This oxymoronic language encapsulates the perplexing character that Christian experience had been found to have. In the New Testament, the problem of how to understand the relationship between the Lordship of Jesus and the Lordship of the one true God of Israel (Deuteronomy 6.4) remains unresolved. The issue is simply present, arising as a fact of experience, encouraged not only by belief in the Resurrection but also by the new life that the first believers found had been given to them in Christ. Paul can only describe the latter as being 'a new creation, everything old has passed away; see everything has become new'. This had become possible because 'in Christ God was reconciling the world to himself, not counting their trespasses against them' (2 Corinthians 5.17–19). Central to Pauline thought is the belief that 'Christ died for our sins in accordance with the scriptures' (1 Corinthians 15.3). The identification of the sinless Jesus with the sinners he came to save is such that Paul has the astonishing boldness to say, 'For our sake [God] made him to be sin who knew no sin, so that in him we might become the righteousness of God' (2 Corinthians 5.21). Even more bluntly, Paul tells the Galatians that 'Christ redeemed us from the curse of the law by becoming a curse for us' (3.13; see also Romans 8.1–4). What human beings could not do for themselves had been done for them in Christ, and this redemption came as a free gift to be received by faith and did not need to be earned by good works (Romans 3.21–26; Galatians 3.1–14). The Pauline witness is absolutely clear, both about the presence of human and divine attributes in Jesus and about the reconciliation (atonement) he has effected between a righteous God and sinful humanity, but in neither case are we given, in Paul or elsewhere in the New Testament, a detailed theological theory of how these things can be. Experience was everything; theorizing could wait. In the case of human/divine duality in Christ, the Church was eventually led to the doctrine of the two natures, proclaimed at Chalcedon in 451, requiring the use of philosophical language quite different from the scriptural style of discourse but, I believe, consonant with scriptural testimony. In the case of the Atonement, the Church, while always witnessing to the fact, has not succeeded in formulating a universally agreed theory.

Another remarkable attribute of Christ that is emphasized by Paul is that, though of course the Christian community knew Jesus was a human individual, it had nevertheless experienced a corporate element in its relationship with Christ. Paul tells the Corinthians that they 'are the body of Christ and individually members of it' (1 Corinthians 12.12–27; see also Romans 12.4–8; Ephesians 4.15–16). He is not using 'body' simply as a simile, but for him it is a spiritual reality. In the ancient world, the image of the body used to represent a community, such as a city, was a common enough figure of speech. However, something altogether more mysterious and counterintuitive is being asserted here. The individual Christians make their individual and indispensable contributions within the integrity of the one body of Christ, which they simply *are*. For Paul, the body of Christ was not a literary device, but a reality. Connected with this is the very frequent use in the Pauline writings of the phrase 'in Christ', which is comparatively rare elsewhere in the New Testament. Examples would be 'the law of the Spirit of life in Christ Jesus has set you free' (Romans 8.2); 'all will be made alive in Christ' (1 Corinthians 15.22); 'you are all one in Christ Jesus' (Galatians 3.28). Without denying the humanity of Jesus, this participatory language points to a reality in him that exceeds the simply human.

It is instructive to see how Paul uses the Hebrew Bible as his scriptural resource. The most systematic of the Pauline letters is Romans, and this provides a good focus for such a study. Sometimes he simply quotes Scripture in a straightforward fashion, as in the long chain of quotations from the Psalms in 3.10–18, but at other times he is much bolder. In 9.33 Paul does not hesitate to fuse two separate verses from Isaiah (8.14 and 28.16), to form a quotation about the stone of stumbling that he wants to use. Most remarkable of all, he feels able to take verses that clearly refer to the Lord God of Israel and apply them to the Lord Jesus Christ. In 10.13, when Paul quotes from Joel, 'Everyone who calls on the name of the Lord shall be saved', the context makes it clear that he is applying this to Christ, while the prophet was obviously referring to the God of Israel. An even more striking example occurs in the 'Christological hymn' of Philippians 2.5–11. It ends with the assertion that 'at the name of Jesus every knee shall bend in heaven and on earth and under the earth, and every tongue confess that Jesus Christ is Lord to the glory of God the Father'. This is an unmistakable echo of what is said about God in Isaiah 45.23. All the more remarkable is the fact that many scholars believe that the apostle is reproducing a pre-Pauline hymn, which would take this form of the proclamation of the Lordship of Christ back into very early times indeed. In Colossians 1.15–20 there is another passage that scholars believe is based on a pre-Pauline Christological hymn. It also speaks of Christ in remarkable terms, calling him 'the image of the invisible God' and asserting that 'he himself is before all things and in him all things hold together'. I shall return to this passage in Chapter 10.

These examples, which have parallels elsewhere in the New Testament, show that the early Church, while respectful of Scripture and wishing to make clear its belief that Jesus fulfilled the expectations and hopes of Hebrew prophecy, felt able to use that Scripture in a manner that was free from a slavish dependence on original use and meaning. It allowed itself to manipulate what had been written in order to conform what was being said to what it had learned by its actual experience of the new life that had been given to it in Christ. There is no warrant in the New Testament for a narrow fundamentalist literalism in our approach to Scripture.

I have referred to 'the Pauline writings' because it is not certain that everything to which Paul's name has been attached was actually written by him. Remember that in the ancient world there was not the modern concept of authorial integrity, so that it was not considered fraudulent to present writing arising in a tradition that stemmed from an original author as if it had actually been written by that author himself. There is general scholarly agreement that Romans, 1 and 2 Corinthians, Galatians, Philippians and 1 Thessalonians are authentic letters by Paul. There are varying degrees of doubt about Ephesians, Colossians and

2 Thessalonians. These epistles show differences of style and content that are apparent when they are compared with the unquestioned letters. However, these variations might have arisen from developments in Paul's thinking, from a different target readership, or even from a different amanuensis, since in all probability the letters were dictated. This is not the place to go into any detail about these issues. I personally have some doubts about Ephesians and more doubts about 2 Thessalonians. There is a separate question about the so-called Pastoral Epistles, 1 and 2 Timothy and Titus. Even a fairly casual reading will show up obvious differences between them and the letters that are addressed to communities. The tone is flatter and the concerns concentrate on organizational matters. One might say that inspiration seems to have given way to routine. Is this because letters to individual Christian leaders will tend to have this character, bearing in mind their responsibilities, or is it a sign that these writings are from a somewhat later period in the Church's history when administrative matters had begun to loom larger? Answering this question is further complicated by the fact that the Pastorals contain a good many apparently personal references (1 Timothy 1.20; 2 Timothy 1.15; 4.9–21; Titus 3.12). A modern author might add these to give the simulation of authenticity, but I doubt that an ancient author would act in this way. Personally I do not quite know what to think about the authorship of the Pastorals. Of course, their place in the canon, and so their authority as Scripture in the Church, does not depend upon Paul having been their actual author.

This chapter has given a very brief survey of matters relating to an important mass of scriptural material. I have only been able to pick out some of the themes and issues that need to be considered. Yet I hope that enough has been presented to persuade the reader of the value of engaging with the rich insights that are to be found in the Pauline writings.

9

Other New Testament writings

In addition to the Gospels and the Pauline writings, there are ten other books in the New Testament. In our brief reconnaissance we do not need to examine every single one, but there are several that require our brief attention.

The first of these is Acts. In its opening verses it addresses someone called Theophilus. Since the name means 'Lover of God', this may well simply refer to the figure of a typical enquirer, rather than being the name of a specific person. Luke's Gospel (1.3) is similarly addressed and almost all scholars agree that the two books are by the same author. This means that Luke was responsible for writing about a quarter of the New Testament. It is significant that he felt the story he had to tell was a two-part drama, with the first act the life, death and resurrection of Jesus Christ, and the second an account of the pouring of the Holy Spirit at Pentecost and the subsequent life and growth of the early Church. There is much less scholarly agreement about when Acts was written. Some suppose it to be in the early 60s, while others date it later, in the 80s. The book ends with Paul having arrived in Rome and having begun teaching there (28.30–31), but it gives no account of his subsequent trial and martyrdom. This suggests to me that these highly significant events had not taken place when the book was written and so I favour an early date.

The dating is relevant to the question of the detailed historical reliability of the story that Acts has to tell, not least in relation to the character of the apostolic witness and preaching that it describes. There is a considerable variety of scholarly opinion about this issue also. Clearly, the earlier the date, the more likely it is that the details are reliable. It seems to me that the account that Acts gives of Pentecost has the ring of truth about it. When Peter addresses the crowd, he says, 'Therefore let the entire house of Israel know with certainty that God has made him both Lord and Messiah, this Jesus whom you crucified' (2.36). The way he puts it sounds very like adoptionism, the theological idea that Jesus was made God's Son at his resurrection because he had been faithful even to the point of accepting death on the cross. However, it was very soon realized in the Christian community that this theory was inadequate, since surely God must have been at work in Jesus in a special way throughout his life, and not simply opportunistically at its end. Hence there soon developed the stronger theory of the sending of the Son, that we find in Paul. This adoptionist tone in Acts 2 suggests to me that the chapter derives from a very early source, near to the events themselves. It is certainly the case that Luke shows an accurate knowledge of the first-century world, giving precise details of the titles of important people and of judicial procedures which can be confirmed from independent secular sources. Acts is very much rooted in the period it purports to be describing and it does not seem to me to have the air of a later imaginative writing. Later in Acts there are several passages written in the first person, the 'We' passages of Acts 16.10–18; 20.6–17; 21.1–18; 27.1—28.16. We know that Luke was a companion of Paul (Colossians 4.14; Philemon 24; see also 2 Timothy 4.11), so it is natural to suppose that he was actually present at the events these passages describe.

The first section of Acts (1—15) has Peter as the principal actor and much attention is focussed on the question of whether gentile converts should be required to submit to Jewish law and custom. The discussion culminates in chapter 15 with an account of the Council of Jerusalem, which imposed just four simple rules for the conduct of gentile Christians (15.19–21). The remainder of Acts has Paul as the principal protagonist, telling the story of his conversion, his three missionary journeys, and his arrest and despatch to appear before Caesar in Rome.

An important New Testament book is the Epistle to the Hebrews. Its author is unknown. (Older English versions often assigned the epistle to Paul, but it is absolutely certain, from considerations of style and theological stance, that this is incorrect.) We shall simply call the author the Writer (most probably male, but this is not completely certain). He had an almost platonic concern with the contrast between the appearance of things, which for him included the Mosaic Law and Jewish worship, and ultimate reality, which is the heavenly status of Jesus. 'When Christ came as a high priest of the good things that have come, then through the greater and more perfect tent (not made with hands, that is, not of this creation), he entered once for all into the Holy Place, not with the blood of goats and calves, but with his own blood, thus obtaining eternal redemption' (9.11–12). The 'tent' is the Tabernacle of the wilderness wanderings, as described in the Pentateuch. The Writer always refers to this tent, rather than to the Jerusalem Temple. Jesus is frequently said to be 'a high priest according to the order of Melchizedek' (5.10; 6.20—7.3; etc.), a reference to Psalm 110.4, and set out in contrast to the nature of the Levitical priesthood that served the Temple (7.11–25). The Writer has a very high Christology: 'in these last days [God] has spoken to us by a Son, whom he appointed heir of all things, through whom he also created the worlds. He is the reflection of God's glory and the exact imprint of God's very being, and he sustains all things by his powerful word' (1.2–3). Nevertheless, the Writer is far from seeing Jesus as a spiritual being who simply appeared to be human. A good deal of the first chapter is devoted to refuting the suggestion that Jesus was an angel in disguise. On the contrary, his full humanity is clearly asserted. We are told that 'it was fitting that God . . . should make the pioneer of their salvation perfect through sufferings. . . . Because he himself was tested by what he suffered, he is able to help those who are being tested' (2.10 and 18). Hebrews 5.7–9 contains the only clear reference to Gethsemane found outside the Gospels.

There is considerable variation in scholarly opinion about the dating of Hebrews. I am personally persuaded that the absence of any reference to the destruction of the Temple in a work which has the transient status of Temple worship as one of its principal themes, means that Hebrews was written before the year 70, when that event occurred. Hebrews is probably one of the books of the New Testament that is among those less familiar to the general reader, but the depth, originality and complexity of its theological discussion surely shows that the Writer was a genius fit to be ranked beside those other two theological geniuses, John and Paul.

A quick survey will suffice for some of the remaining books. The Epistle of James (not the apostle, but quite possibly James the brother of Jesus, who had a very influential role in the early Church in Jerusalem) is a strongly Jewish piece of writing. It is very much concerned with issues of right conduct and the author famously declares that 'faith without works is dead' (2.18–26). This led Martin Luther to call it 'an epistle of straw', but what James is emphasizing is that true faith must be manifested in deeds as well as words.

Although 1 Peter is a genuinely early letter, its sophisticated Greek style makes it unlikely to have come from the pen of the fisherman apostle. One of its principal purposes is to encourage and strengthen a community that is undergoing a 'fiery ordeal' of persecution (4.12–14). On the other hand, 2 Peter is widely believed to be a late work, possibly the latest of all the New Testament writings. It refers to scoffers who say, 'Where is the promise of his coming? . . . all things continue as they were from the beginning of creation' (3.4). Paul's letters seem already to have been collected and are being treated as Christian Scripture (3.15–16).

John's Gospel and 1 John originate in the same school of Christian thinking and they may be by the same author. Many scholars date the epistle subsequent to the Gospel itself. In 1 John, the twin themes of love and light continually reappear and intertwine in a kind of fugue-like composition.

I have said a little about Revelation earlier in Chapter 2, noting its strange character of the alternation of passages of heavenly worship with passages of sadistic punishment. The latter have the crude and repetitive style that makes one think of an animated cartoon. John was a common name in the ancient world and there is absolutely no reason to identify John of Patmos with the author of the fourth Gospel, so strikingly different in its tone. Despite its frequently violent apocalyptic character, Revelation also contains more moderate writing, such as the letters from the risen Christ to the seven churches of Asia (2—3). The book ends with a grand

and inspiring vision of the new Jerusalem, where 'death will be no more; mourning and crying and pain will be no more, for the first things have passed away' (21.4), and where there is 'the river of the water of life, bright as crystal, flowing from the throne of God and of the Lamb' (22.1–2).

10

Profundity

In this final chapter I want to look at three New Testament passages that are of great profundity, and to explore a little of their depth by approaching them from the perspective of a scientist who wishes to locate his understanding of the physical world within the more comprehensive context of wider intelligibility than a theological perspective affords. The discussion will illustrate something of the power of Scripture to continue to foster new insight, even in relation to issues that were completely unknown in the cultural settings in which the Bible originated.

The first of these passages is the Prologue to the Gospel of John:

> In the beginning was the Word, and the Word was with God, and the Word was God. He was in the beginning with God. All things came into being through him, and without him not one thing came into being. What has come into being in him was life, and the life was the light of all people. The light shines in the darkness, and the darkness did not overcome it. . . . He was in the world, and the world came into being through him; yet the world did not know him. He came to what was his own, and his own people did not accept him. But to all who received him, who believed in his name, he gave power to become children of God, who were born,

not of blood or of the will of the flesh or of the will of man, but of God. And the Word became flesh and lived among us, and we have seen his glory, the glory as of a father's only son, full of grace and truth.... No one has ever seen God. It is God the only Son, who is close to the Father's heart, who has made him known.   (John 1.1–5, 10–14, 18)

I have selected here the verses where the evangelist speaks principally from an eternal perspective, and I have omitted some verses that are concerned with a particular historical reference to John the Baptist. This does not imply that these latter verses are not important. In fact, they are of considerable significance, for their reference to a historical episode means they stand in a vital relation to the pivotal verse of the Prologue, which proclaims that 'the Word became flesh and lived among us'. What John has to say concerns eternal truth which is embedded and expressed in historical events. The Prologue speaks of the union of the eternal with the temporal. The Greek word translated 'lived' literally means 'was entented', a reference to the Tabernacle that accompanied the wilderness wanderings of Israel as a covenanted symbol of the divine presence with them. For John, the incarnate Word is the true form of the divine presence with humanity. Already in the Prologue, we encounter the themes of life and light and darkness, which are repeatedly present in the Johannine writings.

To the modern reader John's use of 'Word' (in Greek, *Logos*) may, at first sight, seem strange and puzzling. Its aptness for John's purpose lies in the double reference that it makes to both Greek and Hebrew thinking. Greek philosophers, such as the Stoics, spoke of the Logos as the universal ordering principle of the world. A scientist will immediately think of the deep and wonderful order that physics has discovered to lie at the roots of the universe. Our exploration of the cosmos has revealed that the basic laws of physics are always found to be expressed mathematically in beautiful equations – a property that is related to the economy and elegance of these equations, and one whose presence is something that the mathematicians can recognize and agree about. The equations of physics are remarkably concise as well as beautiful. The physical laws that control the properties of matter in the world of our direct experience (relating to electromagnetism and quantum mechanics) can be expressed in equations that I could literally write down on the back of an envelope. The current quest of theoretical physics is to combine these laws with those that describe other basic forces of nature, such as gravity, to form a Grand Unified Theory of extensive scope and great economy. This ambition has not yet been achieved, but most physicists, myself included, believe that its attainment is a hope that we can reasonably expect eventually to be fulfilled. In its rational transparency and rational beauty, the universe that physics explores could well be described as a world shot through with signs of mind and so it does not seem unnatural to a physicist like myself to believe that it was through the Word that all things came into being.

In Hebrew thinking, Word carried a different connotation. The Hebrew *dabar* means both word and deed and there is a dynamical character to Israel's understanding of 'the word of the Lord' by which the heavens were made (Psalm 33.6). In Genesis 1, God speaks creatures into being by the reiterated command 'Let there be . . .' The opening words of John's Gospel, 'In the beginning', are a conscious echo of the opening words of Genesis.

The fusion of the ideas of enabling order and unfolding dynamic process, suggested by the double linguistic reference of John's use of Word, is highly consonant with science's understanding of cosmic history. The given laws of nature, which are the ground rules for physical process, are not only rationally beautiful, but also had to take a very specific form if the eventual evolution of carbon-based life was to be possible, anywhere or at any time in cosmic history. For example, every atom of carbon in our bodies was made in the nuclear furnaces of the stars. We are literally people of stardust. The process by which this happens is very delicate and it is only possible because the laws of nuclear physics take a very precise, 'finely tuned' form. It took ten billion years for life to appear in our universe, but the cosmos was pregnant with the possibility of life from the very beginning, because its laws took the specific form that was a necessary precondition for life to be able eventually to emerge. Those of us who see the universe as a divine creation will here discern the work of the Word in the Greek sense of Logos. Science also tells us that the potentiality that was already present in the early universe has been brought to actual fruition by a sequence of evolutionary processes, stretching over 13.7 billion years. Here the believer will discern the character of the Word in the dynamic Hebrew sense, for the Creator is to be recognized as acting as much through the unfolding of natural processes, which are expressions of the divine will, as in any other way. We shall return to thinking about evolutionary process later in this chapter.

When Augustine, after his conversion, read the Prologue, he said he found many ideas that were already familiar to him from his days as a pagan philosopher, but when he came to verse 14, speaking of the Word made flesh, he encountered an insight that was without previous precedent for him. Notions of divine order and creative fertility were already familiar, but the Christian concept of the Incarnation, the idea that the Word had truly taken human life, was something entirely new. At the heart of Christianity lies the astonishing, mysterious, exciting, and I believe true, conviction that the infinite and invisible God has acted to make the divine nature known in the clearest and most accessible way, in the Word taking flesh as the man Jesus Christ. This is not the place for me to defend this belief, a task that I have attempted elsewhere (see Further Reading). Instead, I shall turn to another New Testament passage in which a similar kind of startling claim is made, but expressed in a somewhat different manner. Earlier, I briefly referred to the Christological hymn that is part of the opening chapter of the letter to the Colossians:

> [Christ] is the image of the invisible God, the firstborn of all creation; for in him all things in heaven and on earth were created, things visible and invisible, whether thrones or dominions or rulers or powers – all things have been created through him and for him. He himself is before all things, and in him all things hold together. He is the head of the body, the church; he is the beginning, the firstborn from the dead, so that he might come to have first place in everything. For in him all the fullness of God was pleased to dwell, and through him God was pleased to reconcile to himself all things, whether on earth or in heaven, by making peace through the blood of his cross.   (Colossians 1.15–20)

This extraordinary passage is claiming a cosmic significance for Jesus Christ, an assertion that is being made about a person who had been crucified perhaps thirty years before the epistle was written. As in the Prologue to John, it is stated that Christ truly makes known the divine nature as 'the image of the invisible God'. There has been much debate about the meaning of the phrase in Colossians, 'the firstborn of all creation'. The Arian heretics of the fourth century appealed to the phrase to support their claim that Christ was something less than fully divine, a kind of being intermediate between God and all other creatures. Arianism was eventually rejected because of the theological insight that if Jesus is to be our Saviour he must both be truly human (one of us) and truly divine (so that the saving power of God is fully in him). The fact that the passage speaks of Christ as the one in whom 'all things in heaven and earth were created' and that he was 'before all things and in him all things hold together' surely elevates him above solely creaturely status of any kind, indicating that we should understand 'firstborn' as a way of expressing Christ to be prior to and supreme over all creation, which is surely to attribute divine status to him.

What interests me especially in this passage is the last verse which says that Christ reconciles all things by 'making peace through the blood of his cross'. Notice that it is 'all *things*', not simply all people. Redemption is proclaimed to be cosmic in scope. Here is a clear statement that the whole of creation matters to its Creator. The universe is not just there to be the backdrop to the human drama taking place after an overture lasting 13.7 billion years. All creatures have value, and all creatures must have an appropriate destiny of fulfilment. Yet everything in this creation ends in death and futility as far as the story that science can tell is concerned – ourselves on a timescale of tens of years, and the universe itself on a timescale of many billions of years, as continued expansion and the increasing cold and dilution that are its result means that eventually all carbon-based life will disappear from it. Theology has to take this story of inescapable ultimate futility very seriously. The final passage I want to look at addresses this problem, expressed in terms of a first-century understanding of the world.

> For the creation waits with eager longing for the revealing of the children of God; for the creation was subjected to futility, not of its own will but by the will of the one who subjected it, in hope that the creation itself will be set free from its bondage to decay and will obtain the freedom of the glory of the children of God. We know that the whole creation has been groaning in labour pains until now; and not only the creation, but we ourselves, who have the first fruits of the Spirit, groan inwardly while we wait for the adoption, the redemption of our bodies.
>
> (Romans 8.19–23)

Why should God have subjected the creation to futility? There is a resonance here, not only with modern scientific predictions of eventual cosmic futility, but also with the inescapable cost of evolutionary natural process. The way in which creatures are given the gift of being allowed 'to make themselves' (the theological way to understand an evolving creation) not only brings to birth fruits of the fertile potential with which the creation has been endowed, but also has an inescapable shadow side to it. In an evolving world, the death of one generation is the necessary cost of the new life of the next. Genetic mutation not only produces new forms of life to be sifted and preserved through natural selection, but sometimes it is the source of malignancy. Creative processes take place at the 'edge of chaos', where order and disorder interlace. If things were simply tightly ordered, they would be too rigid ever to generate something really new. If they were too haphazard, no novelty that emerged would be able to persist. There has to be enough genetic mutation to produce new forms of life, but not so much mutation that these new forms do not get established as species on which the sifting effects of natural selection can act. Creative processes of this kind will necessarily generate ragged edges and blind alleys as well as extraordinary fruitfulness. In this insight there is some help for theology as it wrestles with the problems of disease and disaster in the divine creation. They are not something gratuitous, that a God who was a bit more competent or a bit less callous could easily have eliminated. They are the inescapable cost of the good of a world in which creatures are allowed to make themselves.

The costliness of evolutionary process means that the creation has indeed been 'groaning in labour pains until now'. However, the last word does not lie with death and futility, but with God. It is the Christian hope and belief that the divine faithfulness will not allow anything of good eventually to be lost, but God will give to all creatures an appropriate destiny beyond their deaths, as the old creation is ultimately transformed in Christ into the new creation. Christians believe that this process has, in fact, already begun in the seed event of the resurrection of Jesus. Paul sets before us the hope and promise 'that the creation itself will be set free from its bondage to decay and will obtain the freedom of the glory of the children of God'. Ultimate cosmic destiny and ultimate human destiny lie together in the One who redeems all things by the blood of his cross. Romans 8 is one of the most profound and hopeful chapters in the New Testament and reading it in the light of modern scientific understanding helps us to find new levels of profundity in it.

Further Reading

First I must recommend two substantial reference works that offer comprehensive and balanced surveys of current scholarly opinion about biblical matters. Both books would be of great assistance to anyone wanting to undertake a serious engagement with the kinds of issues that in our encounter we have only been able to raise and exemplify, without addressing them exhaustively. *The Oxford Companion to the Bible*, ed. B. M. Metzger and M. D. Coogan (Oxford: OUP, 1993), contains more than seven hundred encyclopedia-style articles, dealing not only with the text of the Bible itself and the variety of the cultural settings in which it originated, but also with subsequent historical developments in biblical use and with many contemporary questions of theological and ethical interpretation. The format of *The Oxford Bible Commentary*, ed. J. Barton and J. Muddiman (Oxford: OUP, 2001), is that of a conventional commentary, with introductions to the different sections of Scripture, together with individual commentaries on each of the biblical books, including those classified as Apocrypha, such as the Wisdom of Solomon and the Books of Maccabees, which are included in Catholic Bibles, but usually omitted in Protestant ones because they were written in Greek and not in Hebrew. These individual commentaries first deal with issues such as dating and authorship, style and theological focus, before going on to discuss the text itself, passage by passage. Either or both of these reference books would be an excellent aid to someone wanting to continue and extend a serious study of the Bible. One could say that they provide the main courses of the biblical meal, for which this slim volume has, I hope, been a kind of hors d'oeuvre.

When we come to books addressing more specific and focussed topics, their number is legion. All I can do is to suggest a selection of a few that I believe would be found helpful, even if this is necessarily very much a personal choice. I include several of my own books in the list of those that I propose, not because I have an exaggerated estimate of the importance of my own writing, but because, for obvious reasons, they do fit quite readily into the role of extending what I have had to say here.

On the general character of Scripture, one might look at John Barton, *What is the Bible?* (London: SPCK, 1991). For a more detailed account of my own thoughts, one could turn to Chapter 5 of *Reason and Reality* (London: SPCK, 1991) and Chapter 2 of *Science and the Trinity* (London: SPCK, 2004).

An accessible and careful account of scholarly assessments of the writings of the Hebrew Bible can be found in H. McKeating, *Studying the Old Testament* (London: Epworth, 1979). Similar issues are discussed in J. Rogerson and P. Davis, *The Old Testament World* (Cambridge: CUP, 1989), which pays particular attention to the associated cultural settings in the ancient world. In addition, the book has some excellent photographs of the relevant landscapes. My approach to understanding the Fall is presented in more detail in Chapter 8 of *Reason and Reality*. The book which discusses the Exodus story from a scientific point of view, referred to in Chapter 5, is C. Humphreys, *The Miracles of Exodus* (London: Continuum, 2003).

An interesting introduction to the Gospels is the narrative approach of R. Burridge, which can be found in his *Four Gospels, One Jesus?* (London: SPCK, 2004). Among the numerous books about the historical Jesus, I would like to mention J. Dunn, *A New Perspective on Jesus* (London: SPCK, 2006), and N. T. Wright, *Who Was Jesus?* (London: SPCK, 1992). The quotation from C. F. D. Moule, cited in Chapter 6, is taken from *The Origins of Christology* (Cambridge: CUP, 1977). The quotation about 'binitarian monotheism' in the New Testament (Chapter 8) is taken from L. Hurtado, *Lord Jesus Christ* (Grand Rapids: Eerdmans, 2003). This is a massive scholarly volume, giving a very thorough discussion and defence of the thesis that Jesus was worshipped by his followers from the very earliest days of the post-resurrection Church. Another massive scholarly volume is R. Bauckham, *Jesus and the Eyewitnesses* (Grand Rapids: Eerdmans, 2006), which argues for an important role for actual eyewitness testimony in the formation of the gospel narratives.

The Resurrection is discussed in G. O'Collins, *Jesus Risen* (London: DLT, 1987), and in his *Christology* (Oxford: OUP, 1995). In the latter, O'Collins surveys thinking about the nature of Christ from the earliest New Testament times up to the great Church Councils of the fourth and fifth centuries. A magisterial survey of all issues relating to the Resurrection can be found in N. T. Wright, *The Resurrection of the Son of God* (London: SPCK, 2003).

My own views on these important issues concerning the nature and significance of Jesus, including a discussion of 'The Son of Man', can be found in Chapters 5 to 7 of *Science and Christian Belief* (London: SPCK, 1994); in North America, *The Faith of a Physicist* (Minneapolis: Augsburg Fortress, 1996). My views on miracle can be found in *Science and Providence*

(West Conshohocken, PA: Temple Foundation Press, 2005), Chapter 4. Eschatological issues, referred to briefly at the end of Chapter 10, are much more extensively discussed in my book, *The God of Hope and the End of the World* (London: SPCK, 2002).

Index